THAT THEY MAY BE ONE

AMY OHLER

ISBN: 978-1-7776170-0-4

Cover Art: Copyright @ 2021 Josh Wentz

Editors: Fleur Marie Vaz, Ken Weist, Lara Schroeter

Table of Contents

Preface

I must admit that writing this book was unexpected and has come about more as a step of obedience than anything else really. Quite a number of years ago, a gifted speaker and author visited our little local church community in Turkey. He taught and shared with us for a couple of evenings, and on one of those evenings, he felt God lead him to share some specific words with a couple of people in our congregation, and I was one of those.

The first part of the word this brother shared for me was an accurate picture of my situation, an affirmation that God not only sees my heart's desires but that he is using them to help others encounter him and experience freedom. I was able to receive this part of the word as a direct encouragement to continue moving forward and pressing deeper into a particular area of inner healing ministry I had recently become active in.

The second part of the word, however, did not resonate with me in the slightest. He said that he also felt there would be books coming out of me, that God would show me to write. Now, while I keep a journal (a scattered, messy record of my interactions with God), I do not at all consider myself a writer. I do love books and poetry that speak stirringly of God and of the human condition, and stories that grip and pull you in with their artistry or depth. I have a deep appreciation for talented writers, poets, and lyricists who have the ability to put deep emotions and experiences down onto paper in understandable, relatable, and elegant words. But I have never personally had any real aspirations to write.

Moreover, at that time I did not actually have anything pressing on my heart to communicate to others in writing. And so, I simply set that part of the word aside in my mind. I decided he was maybe amiss in what he thought God was speaking, and so there was no need to consider it any further, unless circumstances should dictate otherwise.

Fast forward a couple of years to a meeting with a few female leaders from the local church and another visiting guest from the States. This guest was part of an organization that has helped connect financial resources from other nations into many different projects in Turkey. This particular guest was specifically interested in projects that were focused on empowering women and having them become more involved in a wider range of ministries. She had a number of questions about our experiences as women in Turkey, both in the church and in general society.

It was an enriching conversation. I realized that, as a westerner living in a partly European, partly Middle-Eastern nation, and as one who is involved in diverse settings in terms of culture and religious beliefs (including a wide range of denominations and traditions), that I had much to share on the subject. As I walked home from the meeting that day, I was overwhelmed with a thousand thoughts running through my head.

So many that I decided I would need to jot them down to process later on. In the days to come I continued to have more thoughts. Scattered and incomplete as they were, I realized that these thoughts were heavy on my heart, ones that I wanted to explore further, and that I wanted to communicate with others. It dawned on me that these thoughts would be good in a book. Then I remembered the word I had been given.

Therefore, this book was initially birthed out of a search to understand the role of women in leadership according to what is revealed in scripture. In this pursuit I have found myself in a variety of church communities and cultural settings as a single in both 'typical' and 'atypical' female roles, never seeking out, but often finding myself in positions of leadership. Through all of this I have tried to figure out my place and role as a woman in a way that honours God as well as the people and contexts in which I find myself. In my various roles in these different settings, I have been met with both positive and negative responses from those within my realms of responsibility. Most of these responses have been reactions to my personality, giftings, weaknesses, or woundings; but some have been reactions specific to my gender.

As I began to dive deeper into conversation with God about the role of women, I found myself heading down an unfamiliar path with new stops. As I travelled further down the path, I soon discovered that my main question—what is the female identity and role?—was not actually the central question to be asked. I began to understand that this cannot be the most pressing question of my life, since it is not a complete one. I began to see that my finite view was much more limited than I had formerly understood. Awe increased as I began to see how beautifully complex we are and the potential weight of glory that humankind carries. I moved from a focus on the female identity and role, to a focus on unity: an exploration of how all of humankind is connected, to each other and also to the God-head, how that is made possible, and yet how little we experience this and why.

Since moving to Turkey, unity has become something of increasing value as much as it has seemed elusive in many of the contexts I have become involved in. Some of the greatest moments of breakthrough I have seen during my sojourn in the Middle East have consistently involved restoration of unity, or purposeful acts done in pursuit of unity. I have seen this happen across racial and national lines, across denominational divides, among church communities, and also in examples of healing and reconciliation within families. There is perhaps nothing more beautiful, while also nothing more difficult or embattled than unity.

As much as I enjoyed beginning to explore this subject of unity by looking deeper into scripture while talking to God about it and drawing upon my experiences, I felt inadequate to take on writing a book. I felt a bit overwhelmed by the task and somewhat confused as to why I should be one to take it on. Yet I felt God confirm that he was in this, that he was indeed inviting me to write and equipping me to do so. And so, I chose to obey and set out to write.

As I began to write, my wonder grew. I became increasingly in awe at the familial nature of the Godhead, and my desire to be fully united with the Father, the Son, and the Spirit became much more acute. I also became increasingly amazed at humankind, stirred by who and what we were meant to be, deeply disturbed by what we have become, but also astounded by what we have been given, are invited into, and are capable of. My desire to be more fully united with those who love God and are called according to his purpose also became so much more acute.

As I continued to write, it became glaringly clear to me that essentially everything God has ever done in this world is so that all may be one. His heart and focus is unity. As such, it became a driving motivation to help others to see God's incredible calling, and his perfect provision for us that we may be healed, whole, reconciled, and unified so that others may know and love him more, and that we may all come into the fullness of his desire. This book is an expression of the wonder I experienced as I engaged with this topic. Its pages overflow with a deep desire for unity, and it is an invitation to the reader to consider the great joy in all of this and to participate in this marvellous act of recreation.

1

May I Never Lose The Wonder

*We can never know who or what we are till we know
at least something of what God is.*
—A. W. Tozer[1]

*Unfathomable Sea!
All life is out of Thee,
And Thy life is Thy blissful Unity...*

*We from Thy oneness come,
Beyond it cannot roam,
And in Thy oneness find our one eternal home.*
—Frederick William Faber[2]

We have been given an incredible gift in the Bible, a story of God at work through people's lives. It is a story that we've been told since childhood for some, only more recently for others. As we read it, we see it's a story which humankind

---

[1] Tozer, A.W. *Knowledge of the Holy*. Bibliotech Press, 2019.
[2] Tozer, A.W. *The Christian Book of Mystical Verse*. Christian Publications, Inc., 1963.

lives out—we see ourselves in it, and identify with the characters—and one we continue to live out, sensing that somewhere our little stories are also being merged into a larger story. And so, we watch expectantly for a fulfilling outcome. It is a story told by multiple voices spanning cultures and generations, telling of what has been, and promising things that are yet to come. It is the story of God and humanity: It is our story. Much of it has been carefully recorded, though not all of it. We have only been given the essential parts, those which lay foundations, maintain continuity of characters and plot, and drive the storyline forward into a sought after resolution. We have been given just enough to invite us into conversation with the author and central character. For those of us who have become over familiar with the story, I have chosen to approach it primarily as a narrative, as if we were coming to it for the first time, in hopes that we will be able to look at it afresh, to discover how the theme of unity is played throughout.

"In the beginning, God created..." The first line recorded of our story begins with a time, a subject, and an action: The beginning. God. Creating. Before we move past the very first paragraph, before we have a chance to puzzle over the presence of evil, dismay over disease or natural disasters, debate about when or how our end will come, before we are even mentioned in the story, we are told of God. Well, 'Gods' actually, since the word in this first line is *Elohim*, the plural form of *El* (or *Eloah*) the Hebrew word for God. It is a detail we tend to gloss over, and rightly so, since verb conjugation and pronouns used with *Elohim* are generally singular not plural; also because when asked later on, *Elohim* gives Moses a single, specific name YHWH,[3] and because throughout the story God is declared to be *one*.[4] Thus when we return and read the story from the beginning, we contentedly read *Elohim* as 'God' not 'Gods'. And yet, here, already in the first line of the story, a little of the mystery of this God so central to our faith is offered.

Who and what is this God? Why does he create? What does it matter to us? We can begin by answering the last question—it matters because our story originates with this God. Knowing the nature and purpose of the source of all that we currently see, are, and experience is key to understanding why and how we are here, who we are, and where we are going. To answer the other questions, more than just a line or two is needed. Join me in becoming a child for a little while in order to dive into this mystery and see what we might find.

"In the beginning God created the heavens and the earth."[5] From the first line of our story, we understand that God existed before us and made all that we now dwell in. But that is all we are given. We aren't told of God's story before us; we aren't told why or how he *is*. That riveting piece of information, unfortunately, isn't recorded here or anywhere else. Knowing why and how God exists would be a desperately interesting story but it has been left out; therefore it simply must not be paramount to the story we currently find ourselves in. Our story—begins with God creating.

In the beginning we have God making things, really spectacular things, making *all* things. Why? We are left to guess,

---

[3] Exodus 3:14 *Though YHWH is used even in the second chapter of Genesis already.*

[4] Deuteronomy 6:4

[5] Genesis 1:1

but since we, too, have been given the capacity to create, we do have some frame of reference within which to pose an answer to this. We can imagine ourselves in his place and think why we might create. We create for the sheer joy of it, the delight of bringing something new and unique into existence. We create in order to express ourselves, putting our personality, preferences, or uniqueness on display so others can know us. We create to bring pleasure or to stir up a reaction in others, or to receive praise or admiration from them. Sometimes we create in order to try to fulfil a need or to improve a circumstance.

Could it be that God might have created for such reasons as well? Was he exhilarated and delighted at making things out of nothing? Could it be that God would want to express himself or put himself on display? Could it be that he would want to bring pleasure to another or to receive admiration from them? Could it be that there is a need he desires to fulfil or a circumstance that he wants to improve after he begins creating? I believe that our story begins with the words "God created" to let us know that the author expresses and reveals himself, desires to improve and expand on what is, and seeks to draw a response, bring joy, and receive admiration, both to and from himself, but also to and from the ones the story is written for and about.

In looking at the creation account given in Genesis it seems that God is so unique, so *other,* that an entire universe is needed in order to provide even a remote idea of who and what this being is. Could it be that in creating the universe, God desired to give physical expression of himself in order to allow physical beings to know him? Could it be that this world God gave us is interlaced with parables and metaphors that were made to reveal him? The universe is an astonishingly complex, intricate expression and reflection of the One who conceived of it. Think just how massive the One who designed and shaped this universe has to be. Larger than me, of course, larger than a blue whale or the nation of Canada, certainly larger than the earth or any other planet for that matter, larger than every star, every solar system, every galaxy, larger than all of these combined…and then even larger still.

But it gets better. Not only is God larger than the universe, he is also smaller than it. Embedded in the phrase "God created the heavens and the earth" is the idea that he is both inconceivably large but also immeasurably small. He made things so tiny that they have only recently been identified by humankind through the development of incredible technology. God designs and shapes cells, DNA, atoms, neutrons, quarks (and whatever smaller things we still have yet to discover). Is the God of our story both small enough to shape DNA but also large enough to shape a galaxy? Does time have any meaning for a being who is at once present in the galaxy farthest from ours while also right where I am, or you are at this exact moment? Do boundaries exist for a being somehow simultaneously so large and so small? My mind is not actually capable of processing, let alone grasping such ideas. I can really only sit in awe.

Let's continue with the story. "The Spirit of God was hovering over the face of the waters."[6] We've been briefly introduced to God, to the heavens and the earth, and now we are told of water. Water, without doubt, is one of the most fascinating substances we've ever encountered. In its purest form

[6] Genesis 1:2

as a liquid (or as a gas) it is practically colourless, odourless, tasteless, and shapeless, yet incredibly powerful. Water overcomes fire, splits rock when force is applied (or when it changes from a liquid to a solid in or around rock), and effortlessly carves deep canyons in stone over time. Water is found in every living thing; without it there is no life. It surrounds, it fills, it moves, it carries, it penetrates, it cleanses, it refreshes, it cools, it softens. We can dive into and swim through it, but also ride on top of it. We can eat, drink, and breathe it. What do these characteristics communicate to us about the One who created such a miraculous substance?

Scripture is filled with examples that liken God—who he is and what he does for us—to water and its place and function in our lives. For example, we metaphorically drink from the fountain of life, we are submerged in water as we partake of the death of Jesus in baptism, and we talk about being washed clean from sin. The imagery of water in connection with God has continued into the language of today in images such as 'soaking prayer' or being 'immersed' in his presence. These metaphors help us make better sense of God. But God does not simply use images and elements from our world to aid us in our understanding; no, he actually *creates* the metaphors.

Let's look at another created metaphor. "And God said, 'Let there be light.'"[7] Here we are introduced to light, well, essentially we are introduced to fire, since the sun and the stars are massive spheres of burning gases. Fire is as remarkable and mystical a substance as water. I invite you to put the book down for a moment. Go and get a candle, light it, and take a moment to observe the flame and experience its effects. See how it

[7] Genesis 1:3

moves and twists, how the colours mix amidst the glow, how it illuminates, and how it warms. Fire is essentially formless; you cannot grasp or hold onto it, and even when contained it still twists and moves freely. Fire requires a spark to exist and fuel to continue. When much fire is gathered in one place (such as the sun), it is difficult, even dangerous, for us to look directly at it; yet by it, we are able to see everything else. If we get too close to it, we can be irreparably damaged, even destroyed, but at a safe distance we are made comfortable and kept protected. Through the use of heat from fire, other substances are dramatically transformed. Some are improved, as when dough becomes bread, while others are destroyed, as when a tree becomes ash. Some are neither altered nor destroyed but purified, as when silver or gold become free of impurities. Without fire, there would be no life since there would be no warmth in the universe and nothing would move, and since there would be no light to see our way. What do these characteristics of fire reveal to us about the One who created it? Consider how often in scripture God is compared to fire as a means to understand his nature and ways, and remember that he created this metaphor to reveal something of himself.

"And God said, 'Let there be an expanse.'"[8] We have been introduced to the heavens, the earth, the waters, light (or fire), and now we are introduced to the 'expanse'— to air really. Air takes its place alongside water and fire in creating wonder. We cannot actually see, taste, or touch air, and for a long time we only knew of its existence by observing its effects. We feel air blow across our face and fill up our lungs, and we see it move the branches of the trees and form bubbles in water. We rarely

[8] Genesis 1:6

think about air; seldom are we consciously aware of its presence, but should there ever be a change in its make-up, or a lack of it, the impact would be immediate and severe, and we would think of nothing else. While air is nearly imperceptible to us (though we are engulfed by it everywhere we go), it can generate pressure strong enough to lift and carry an airplane full of people, whip water into a destructive funnel, or tear apart massive buildings. A force unseen and yet necessary for life, both impalpable, yet extraordinarily powerful. What can we surmise about the One who designed such a substance?

The creation story continues, and we are told of vegetation, of the moon and stars for the measurement of time, of birds, of sea creatures, of creepy crawlies, and of land animals of all shapes and sizes. If I were to stop here to wonder at each of the above-mentioned, this book would never end. There are not enough encyclopaedias, not enough *National Geographic* specials, not enough episodes of *Our Planet* to even begin to explore the astounding complexity and beauty of the earth we find ourselves dwelling in.

The inexplicable order and unity of ecosystems in a wide variety of environments, along with the intensely beautiful, occasionally grotesque, yet always perfectly adapted plants, insects and animals that dwell in them, invite us into a lifetime of contemplation of the nature and character of the One who so perfectly and deliberately fashioned them. What do we understand of the Creator of mountains, of soil, of sand? Of well over 20,000 different species of orchids? Of the cactus, the oak tree, or bioluminescent algae? Of the ant, the deep sea anglerfish, the platypus, the sheep, the lion, or the eagle? Often we marvel at what we observe in nature, yet we can also be confused, sometimes disturbed by what we see. Regardless, contemplation of the natural world is always an invitation to conversation, to meet and dialogue with the One who made it all.

The story that we find ourselves in tells about the creation by breaking it up into parts, using days as markers. The first three days involve the creation of broad categories and the following three days the creation of those things which fit within those broad categories. He forms, and then he fills what has been formed. Day one we are introduced to light, and day four we are told that light takes the shape of stars and the moon for measuring times and seasons. Day two we are introduced to the sky and the waters, and day five to everything that dwells in them. Day three we are told of the land and all vegetation that springs up from it, and then day six of those that will occupy the land and consume the vegetation. It is clear that the pieces fit together into a whole.

On day six, after the universe has been created and ordered—every piece in it strategically placed—the last piece is introduced. Humankind finally enters the scene. It is interesting to note that in the telling of this story humans do not simply get lumped together with the rest of the living creatures brought forth from the earth. While of course unique, we could argue that humans are essentially just animals; we technically belong to the same category and really should just be a side note in the creation story. Presumably, it would have been sufficient to imply our creation as part of all the living creatures that were brought forth from the earth on day six. But clearly it was not—not in this story. The creation of humankind is given a separate place in Genesis chapter one, and then also given a more detailed description in chapter two. It seems that something unique is being revealed in humankind.

On the sixth day the telling of the creation of humankind begins with slightly different language than that which is used for the telling of every other aspect of creation. Usually the telling begins with a verb connected to the created, such as 'Let there be', 'Let the earth sprout', or 'Let the waters swarm', but the telling of the creation of humankind begins with a verb connected to God, 'Let us make'. God *commands* most of creation but he *makes* humans. 'Making' implies touch, interaction, and process. Such language hints at the personal investment God has in the creation of humankind. Man was intimately crafted by God.

"Then God said, 'Let us make man in our image, according to our likeness; let them have dominion'...God created man in his own image, in the image of God he created him, male and female he created them."[9] Such a unique interplay between plural and singular forms here in these sentences. The text goes between *us* and *him*, then *our* and *his* for God. Then similarly, *man* is first followed with the pronoun *them* while later followed with the pronoun *him*. Then *man* is explained as *male and female* followed by the pronoun *them*. In the text we are given no immediate, clear explanation as to why this is, and why only here and nowhere else in the creation story. My sense is that here we are offered another subtle hint about the nature of this God we will get to know better as the story continues on, and a subtle hint about the reason why humankind receives a separate place in the creation story. It seems that God is one but also somehow more than one, and humans are clearly more

[9] Genesis 1:26-27

than one, but also somehow one. In verse twenty-eight of Genesis one, God blesses the man and the woman, and speaks to them. The first thing he says is, "Be fruitful and multiply." It is in their make-up and in their manifold to unite to bring forth others, and from the others, more unions, and then still more others, eventually a vast population. When God creates male and female, he has actually created all of humankind, for in them lies all who are to come. The image of God is not just male and female, not just individual, but it is the *entirety* of humankind.

In the first few paragraphs of the creation story, we see unfolding before us the mystical, intangible God giving physical form and expression to attributes of who and what he is. We see tangible expressions of his immensity and power, his omniscience and abundance, his beauty and intricacy, his order and perfection, and his character and nature in that which is created in the first twenty-five verses of Genesis chapter one. But there is yet still more to be given expression to, perhaps the most important aspect of this incredible being we know as God. Intelligence was given to humankind—the capacity to analyze, to create, to problem solve, and to dream—important but not the most important piece. Rulership was a divine mandate given to humankind, which reveals something of the Creator, but this is not the most important aspect either. The ability to communicate using language was given to humankind—the ability to remember history, and to speak of the future—while a tremendous capacity, it is not the most vital. I believe that what God wanted to reveal and to experience through the creation of humankind was relationship. Being created in the image of God means having the capacity to experience and demonstrate love.

In chapter two of Genesis we get a second more detailed account of the creation of humankind. Since what was created in this second account seems to be in a different sequence compared with the first, we can assume that the first account of creation is perhaps more representational than chronological. The focus in chapter one is the form, order, and unity of the larger universe; in chapter two the focus is on humankind and their unique place in the story.

We are told God forms man and then breathes life into him. God shapes him by hand and then breathes life into him in an almost uncomfortably intimate fashion. Such unique care is put into this particular creation. Man comes alive and then God brings each of the animals before him. Man gets a good long look at the whole amazing wild kingdom, long enough to come up with an appropriate name for each creature. Can you imagine the wonder of that scene, man discovering—for the first time ever—each and every fantastic creature that God has thought up? Each animal, uniquely glorious, perfectly suited to its environment and, to some extent, relational. But man recognizes that none of them is the right companion for him.

We are told that God has man sleep and then takes a rib from him. Out of that rib God forms something new, woman. We presume the same care and attention has been taken in shaping the woman and breathing life into her as was taken with the man. I wonder if in that moment God was excitedly anticipating man's reaction to seeing woman for the first time. When man does awake and sees the woman, he exclaims, "This at last is bone of my bones and flesh of my flesh!"[10] Finally, after all the stunning creatures man has beheld and named, here is one who is actually *of* him. This is one he can relate to, one he can bond and unite with, one he can love in the way he was designed to love, and one who can reciprocate this love, for she, too, has been created with the same capacity.

Following this beautiful scene we read this statement, "Therefore a man shall leave his father and his mother and hold fast to his wife, and they shall become one flesh."[11] This statement is certainly emphasizing the profound union of male and female, but it is also adding something more to the picture, something bigger than either of them. Thus far in the story we have been introduced to man and woman, but right here we are introduced to two new terms, *mother* and *father*. Here lies some mystery. Inherent in the term *mother* is both father and child. Inherent in the term *father* is both mother and child. Inherent in the term *child* is both mother and father. In every union there is more than a duo, there is actually a trio. Every single individual who has ever lived is uniquely bound to at least two others. This is true even if they are adopted, or a product of in vitro fertilization, every individual requires the existence of at least two others, and is significantly affected by them even if they never meet. Each one of us is a living, moving representation of a trio. Even the first man and woman were living, moving representations of the divine trio.

Every person carries something of their mother, something of their father, but is also their own person. If they choose to leave their mother and father to unite with someone and bring

[10] Genesis 2:23
[11] Genesis 2:24

about another, that new person will carry something of that union but will also be something very distinct from it. This gives pause for thought. Our identity is certainly informed and shaped by the community in which we find ourselves when we begin our lives, but it is also informed and shaped by biology. Many of our physical attributes and characteristics are given to us by our parents, and research has shown that much of our emotional make-up and personality is also dictated by our biological family, not just our social environment or our personal choices. Who we are is determined through a delicate dance between biology, relationship, circumstance, and choice. We are not independent little creatures.

I recently stumbled on a short BBC news report about a young woman born by a sperm donor who had signed up to be reachable should the children born by his donations ever desire to connect. She reached out, and in doing so she discovered that she had many siblings she had known nothing of. The siblings featured in this news report were all very grateful to get to know those to whom they had a blood connection with, and all planned to continue those relationships, even if uncertain as to what those relationships would look like. They all shared a desire for connection; they all wanted to know where they came from, who they belonged to, and who belonged to them.

One girl in the video shared that she had been a double donor conception, meaning that both the sperm and the egg in her conception had been donated. As such she had known neither of her biological parents. She had been wanted and loved by her non-biological parent, of course (hence the effort gone into bringing her into the world), yet she described having felt like an alien, as if she had been forced onto the earth. In the news report we see her hug one of the half siblings she had just been introduced to, and then describe hugging him as some sort of 'homecoming'. None of the siblings featured in the report showed any kind of dissatisfaction with their given families but all described the joy of an unexpected deep connection they felt to one another. We are designed such that we sense and long for connection to those who share our blood, our DNA.

The mother-father-child mix is the most base level of the 'structure' of humankind. Included in the larger scheme are grandparents, siblings, aunts, uncles, and cousins. Then there are in-laws with all the extensions that they bring, and there are also step families through multiple marriages or multiple partners. In the larger scheme there are also children born out of rape, prostitution, or any number of other undesirable circumstances. The connections are not always consistent, and certainly not always good, but they are always there. Reaching up from these base levels of connection, we then have tribes, nations, and entire races. The fact is, whether we like it or not, or perhaps whether we like *them* or not, we are inextricably linked to others, a whole pack of others. God created humans as individuals but also humankind as a whole. We are many but also somehow one.

We are completely bound up with one another. Our personalities are dramatically impacted by others, as the personalities of others are dramatically impacted by us. In an ideal world, these communities—small and large—would be splendid examples of self-giving, joyous, life-long commitment. But as we all know, we are living in a less than ideal world.

2

Things Are Not Okay Right Now

*The work of restoration cannot begin until
a problem is fully faced.*
—Dan B. Allender[1]

Man is the only creature who refuses to be what he is.
—Albert Camus[2]

In the next part of the story, God places first the man, and then the woman in the garden he has prepared so that they can care for it and also be cared for. Everything they need to enjoy their life is found there, fully available to them. Something called the tree of life is there, totally accessible, any time they want. Something called the tree of the knowledge of good and evil is also there, totally accessible, any time they want. The presence of these two trees in the story tells us that the man and the woman have available to them the choice of life. They

[1] Allender, Dan B. *The Wounded Heart: Hope for Adult Victims of Childhood Sexual Abuse.* Colorado Springs, CO: NavPress; 1995.
[2] Camus A. *The Rebel.* London: Penguin Books; 2013.

also have the choice to decide for themselves a standard of what is right and what is wrong. These two choices are opposing, because the second choice is actually a decision to step away from the source of all life.

God warns them against eating from the tree of the knowledge of good and evil. He lets them know the result would be death—meaning total and complete separation from him, the source of life. He warns them of the dire consequences; but he does not remove the option from them. For love to exist, the kind of love that we see in the Godhead, there must be freedom to choose, freedom to reject; otherwise it is not love. In order for love to be voluntary, there must be the option not to choose it. In warning the man and woman not to eat from the tree of the knowledge of good and evil, God is inviting them to allow him to determine the standard of good and evil. It is an invitation to trust his love, to believe that he has their best interests at heart.

As the story continues, the woman (and the man who is with her) hears another voice who questions the character and intentions of God. This voice comes from a creature of flesh like them. We are introduced to a serpent, which is to become a symbol of temptation and of danger throughout the story. Strangely, the first humans chose to listen to this voice and not to the voice they knew. In that moment, they did not trust what God said to be true, meaning they did not believe, and so did not reciprocate his love. Before the man and woman even ate from the tree, they had already decided for themselves what is right and what is wrong. The woman looked at the tree and decided the fruit was good, a delight to the eyes, desired to make one wise.[3] So she and her husband ate of it. Immediately there was separation from the source of life. The man and woman suddenly felt fear and shame, two of the most powerful dividing forces known to us. They had chosen the created over and above the Creator. All of humankind (who then were still contained inside the man and the woman) have since chosen this same path. We have all chosen to decide for ourselves the standard of good and evil, and so we have all made a choice for the created, a choice for the flesh. It is a choice to not surrender, trust, or remain connected with God. The results have been, and continue to be, devastating.

You may ask what is so wrong with deciding for ourselves what is good and what is not? If we were created in the image of this amazing God, this God of life and of love, then surely we should have the capacity for properly deciding what is good, should we not? Yes, the capacity is there; God has definitely written eternity on our hearts and has graced us with a good conscience. But that conscience is limited. Why? Because we are. That conscience is significantly impacted by external incidents interacting with internal decisions. We only see our tiny piece in the puzzle. We do not, and indeed cannot, see the big picture. In any given situation we do not see the full impact of our actions, be they upon ourselves, or people around us, or upon future generations, or upon the environment. We aren't that big and we aren't that smart.

We also do not see the consequences of our actions upon God. We see only our immediate needs, wants, desires (and possibly those of the ones we love) and seek to fulfil them as easily and quickly as possible, often not consciously. All the

[3] Genesis 3:6

while, we do not understand that we belong to God and to one another, that our choices deeply impact the whole, for good and for bad. Leaving us to decide for ourselves what is right and wrong means we cease to listen to or trust the only One who can and does see the entire picture, at all times, and from every possible angle. It is a choice to look to the created rather to the Creator.

The first man and woman certainly had no idea how far-reaching the impact of their actions would be, though they got a small glimpse through their first offspring. They brought forth a son and called him Cain, and then another son, Abel. We see that these two men were in communication with the Creator as their parents had been. We are told that they brought him offerings, and so we assume they were told how they could approach God even in the state of separation inherited from their parents. Cain and Abel both prepared offerings for God but it seems that somewhere along the way Cain had missed, or disregarded, something in the instructions: he approached God with an offering that God did not accept. Cain's immediate response to this situation was anger and gloom. It is a response which revealed his perception of God—that God is not good, that he does not have Cain's best interests at heart. It seems that Cain, like his mother and father, had been listening to another voice besides the Creator's. Cain did not come to God to ask the reason his offering was dismissed. No, he had already decided for himself that it *was good* and therefore it *should have* been accepted.

But even when Cain did not come to God, God came to Cain. He asked him why he was angry and sad, and explained that, if Cain does good, then he *will be* accepted. This was a wonderful promise and again a simple invitation to look to God for the standard of good. He then warned Cain that, if he does not do good, then something called sin is crouching at the door waiting for him. This something has desire for him. This was a warning that sin (a coming against divine order, a deciding for oneself what is good) wants to master Cain, but that he must rule over it. If only in that moment Cain had simply turned and said to God, "Okay, so how exactly do I do that?"

But that was not Cain's response. In the very next sentence, we are told that Cain indeed let sin master him. He allowed feelings of jealousy and injustice to overtake him, and he killed his brother. He did not first seek God out to assess the validity of his feelings, or to find a way to overcome them—no, Cain decided what was good in his own eyes, and in doing so, let sin give birth to death. The firstborn of man and woman killed the second born.

Like Cain, we are often blind to how our attempts to alleviate pain, fear, hunger, discomfort, rejection, or shame can cause suffering to others, and in the end, do not actually even fully alleviate our own condition. Much later on in this story, James, a servant of Jesus, writes this for us, "What causes fights and quarrels among you? Don't they come from your desires that battle within you? You desire but do not have, so you kill. You covet but you cannot get what you want, so you quarrel and fight."[4] We want and we desire, sometimes so intensely that we do whatever seems necessary to obtain it, not considering, or perhaps outright ignoring the cost to others or to ourselves.

---

[4] James 4:1-2a NIV

It is important to take a moment to point out that desire—having needs and wants—is not actually a bad thing: we were designed this way. We come into this world as entirely dependent little beings, with a mass of needs. Psychologist Abraham Maslow, well known for his hierarchy of needs theory, observed that all people have needs which exist on a hierarchy in terms of priority. Those needs on the lower levels must be met in order for us to be alive, while the ones at the top must be met in order for us to be fully human. We have physiological needs (air, water, food, sleep, shelter, etc.), the need for security, the need for love and belonging, the need for esteem and, finally, the need for self-actualization. Every single one of these needs, including the physiological ones, must be met through others. We come into the world as babies, initially incapable of providing for any of our needs, physiological or otherwise, and as we move up Maslow's hierarchy, we see that all of the needs are relational in nature. Clearly we are bound to one another. God planned it this way.

Problems first arise when we fail to recognize that we *have* needs which must be met. Problems also arise when we try to have those needs and desires met in something other than our relationship with God or without referencing him in having those met needs through human relationships. Then problems certainly arise when we try to take what we need or want from others without considering *their* needs or desires. Basically, problems arise when we try to relate with one another in ways outside of the standards given by God. "You do not have because you do not ask God,"[5] says James. When we do not come

---

[5] James 4:2b NIV

to God for answers to the desires that engulf us, we cut ourselves off from the source of life, and we miss the blessing.

Sometimes we do finally see that God is the only one who can truly provide for us what we need, and so we come. But even then we can be disappointed. James wisely notes that, "When you ask, you do not receive, because you ask with wrong motives, that you may spend what you get on your pleasures."[6] When we do not come to God in surrender, still choosing to have the final say on what is good and evil, when we do not come to God with the understanding that being whole and healthy is to also meet the needs of others, then we do not come in a posture where we could receive anything from God. For him to answer us when we are in that place would benefit us nothing. It would only serve to reinforce the walls of separation we have already been building (consciously or not). We need the understanding that to come to God is an act of vulnerability and surrender, because it requires us to admit that we are *needy*, and to actually allow God into those empty places. It also means allowing others to come into those places, since God's provision is almost exclusively through other human beings. The reason we must come to God to have *our* needs met is in order that we may be made whole and thus better able to help others have *their* needs met, too. The presence and acknowledgement of need opens the way for an ongoing intimate exchange. It paves a path for real love.

The choice to have needs met in any other way than what God has provided is ultimately a choice for the flesh. It means refusing to connect to the Spirit, the source of life, and thus to

[6] James 4:3 NIV

refuse real love. James calls us adulterous when we choose anything outside of God, saying that he "jealously longs for the spirit he has caused to dwell in us." The central problem is separation—humankind refusing connection, refusing to surrender back to God the spirit he breathed into us in the beginning.

When we think of evil, we generally begin by thinking about devastation on a grand scale—human trafficking, genocide, war, slavery, gang violence, organized crime, corruption, dictatorships, etc.—but such devastation starts out so much smaller than that. It begins with brokenness in individuals, layer upon layer, who have chosen to decide for themselves what is right and what is wrong. Macro devastation begins with the micro. When we fail to represent and reflect the Godhead on the most basic level, by refusing to give or receive love, the effects ripple out to a scale beyond imagination. Something which may seem so small has the potential to become almost uncontainable. A woman ignored and rejected, a man mocked and belittled, a child unseen and unloved, these are the breeding grounds for the widespread brokenness we see all around us.

The book of Judges is for me an example of one such escalation. The last few chapters[7] tell a tale of such degradation as to make my stomach turn. In it we see a prime example of widespread devastation that begins in the small things. The story begins with a Levite passing through a town in the tribe of Benjamin with his concubine and servant. It continues with the rape and murder of the concubine at the hand of some men in the city. It ends with the women and children of the tribe of Benjamin being slaughtered by the other tribes of Israel, and

[7] Judges 19-21

the tribe of Benjamin nearly wiped out entirely. As I engage with this story I can't help but notice how many scenes there are along the story line, where things could have been set right before they got so much worse. There are so many small moments where the story could have been rewritten to end in something other than horrific violence and bloodshed.

What had gone wrong? Had the Levite in the start of this story chosen to have a wife that he loved and cherished rather than a concubine, who he felt he owned, perhaps he would not have been on this whole journey in the first place trying to retrieve her from her father's home. Had someone in Gibeah taken the Levite and those with him into their home when they first arrived at the city square, perhaps they would not have been spotted by trouble-making men out late at night. Had the men who surrounded the old man's home had loved ones that expected them home, or had they not been out late selfishly looking for trouble, then perhaps they never would have come to the old man's home in the first place. Had the old man not offered his virgin daughter and the Levite's concubine, but instead remained as a wall between them and the men at his door, perhaps the men would have been ashamed to attack one of their own; perhaps they would have given up on the effort and left. Had any others in the city heard the cries of a woman being violated and beaten all night long and gone to intervene, perhaps she would have still been alive in the morning.

Had the Levite not been so obsessed with his own honour and desire for revenge, had he not so gruesomely dismembered his dead concubine in order to garner support for revenge, perhaps there would not have been war. Had the city willingly handed over to justice the men who had raped and killed a woman and also threatened to rape a man (and one who was a guest in their town), perhaps there would not have been war. Had the tribes been willing to sit down in council together to find a peaceable method to restore honour and peace, then perhaps there would not have been war. Had the men of the other tribes not brashly vowed to withhold their daughters from the tribe they had just nearly annihilated, then perhaps another town would not have been destroyed and its virgin women not been taken captive. Had anyone, at any point in this story, actually chosen to go to God in humble surrender, to ask him how they should respond to bring glory to him, and thus peace, honour, and life to them, it could have read differently. But it doesn't, because in those days, "everyone did what was right in his own eyes."[8]

This story feels extreme because it is, and yet this pattern of operating according to what we feel is right in our own eyes is all around us. Where I currently live is certainly no exception. Many news stories come to mind, and I'll share just two. One was a report of a double stabbing that had taken place between neighbours in Istanbul. The conflict began with a disagreement between two housewives over the care of neighbourhood street cats near their apartment building; the conflict escalated until the husbands became involved and ended up stabbing one another. Another was the report of a wedding party in Adana ending in tragedy with more than one death and many injuries. The start of that conflict? A child from one family had stepped on the toes of a child from another family on the dance floor. These examples are just as extreme as the story from the book of Judges, and they are current. While we may not have

[8] Judges 17:6, 21:25

personally seen or experienced anything quite like this, I imagine we have all heard of, witnessed, or perhaps even experienced escalation ending in violence that happens in moments of road rage, the aftermath of a sporting event, or in domestic disputes. We really haven't changed.

Perhaps these examples may still feel too extreme or too far removed for some of us. But how many of us have experienced the pain of divorce? Divorce is a prime example of people operating according to what they see as right in their own eyes, consistently making decisions with limited understanding of self, the other person, or of God. This leads to brokenness instead of deepening connection, to division instead of unity. Expectations are assumed rather than communicated, and often are not evaluated objectively. Genuine needs often go unmet because they are unseen and/or are being demanded from the wrong source. This, of course, leads to feelings of fear, rejection, and shame. The couple then tends to react out of places of hurt and self preservation, which only creates more hurt, more walls, and intensifies feelings of fear, rejection, and shame. On the other hand, when we invite God as well as neutral parties into situations like this, so many small decisions along the way can be made which could mitigate outcomes for couples and families drowning in very real hurt and brokenness.

I was recently asked to get involved with a couple here considering divorce. I was glad they had come to a place where they accepted that something was seriously wrong and that things could not, and indeed should not, continue as they were. I wish I could report that they were willing to still try to push through to repair and restoration. This was not the case because each chose to do what was right in their own eyes. Thankfully, all is not lost since each has been open to receive counsel and prayer, each has been willing to really look at themselves and is continuing in a process of healing and growth, though separately. Together with counsellors and wise mentors, they can examine their needs and expectations before God and begin to repent for their part in the problems that led to divorce. Each has been surprised as God has led them to places of hurt from their past, showing them how these places still dramatically impact their present, and affect not only their expectations of others but also their willingness to give to others. Each has begun to receive healing from God as he speaks truth to their spirits about their needs, their limitations, their capabilities, and their true identities. It is my prayer for each of them as individuals to experience wholeness, and my dream that perhaps one day unity could even still be restored in that relationship.

When we do not stop to consider how much we are functioning according to our accepted (or created) standards of good and evil, we are caught up in a cycle of hurt, and wonder why things don't seem to get better. The prophet Isaiah tells us, "Woe to those who call evil good and good evil, who put darkness for light and light for darkness, who put bitter for sweet and sweet for bitter! Woe to those who are wise in their own eyes, and shrewd in their own sight...they have rejected the law of the LORD of hosts, and have despised the word of the Holy One of Israel."[9] Woe to one who uses another for his own pleasure, for both the used and the user are left damaged and empty. Woe to those who criticize and belittle so they can feel

[9] Isaiah 5:20-21, 24

better; they end up hurting others and the encouragement they so crave becomes more elusive. Woe to those who rage in order to feel secure; they seek to protect but the cost is so much more than any perceived gain. Woe to those who try to decide for themselves what is right. There is only heavy sorrow awaiting those who are wise in their own eyes.

Whether a perpetrator of evil or a victim of it, if someone does not come to the source of all life to overcome their circumstances, there is only woe ahead. We did not design and shape the universe. We did not give order to chaos. We did not give meaning and purpose to all that is. We did not make us. So who are we to consider ourselves wise enough to decide what is good and what is not in any given situation? There is only One who can determine this, because there is only One who is good and he has good plans and good counsel. He can and will show us how to change the course of events to bring about life and beauty instead of violence and destruction, if only we would come to him.

3

Bid Thou Our Sad Divisions Cease

When the human race neglects its weaker members,
when the family neglects its weakest one – it's the
first blow in a suicidal movement.
—Maya Angelou[1]

There are only two kinds of people in the end: those
who say to God, "Thy will be done," and those to whom
God says, in the end, "Thy will be done."
—C.S. Lewis[2]

The consequences of taking from the tree of the knowledge of good and evil versus the tree of life were immediate and severe. The first man and woman suddenly felt fear, shame, and guilt in the presence of their Creator and in the presence of one another. They withdrew from connection, trying to hide from God, and they also broke connection, blaming

---

[1] Kelly, Ken. "Angelou: A Celebrated Poet Issues a Call to Arms to the Nation's Artists." *Mother Jones Magazine*, May-Jun 1995, Vol. 20, No. 3.
[2] Lewis, C. S. *Great Divorce*. Harpercollins Publishers, 2012.

one another. Division became their new reality and it is what we inherited and now walk in.

We are divided—divided from God, divided from creation, divided from one another, and divided even within our own souls. Division is problematic because it assumes an original coherent whole; it means there is a breaking off from something much larger and much more complete. Without an overarching perspective on what the whole was, or is to be, division only serves to tear apart, leaving damaged pieces in its wake. Division in the hands of finite humankind is decidedly destructive.

Division in the hands of the Creator, though, is quite the opposite. We witness that in the creation process, DNA and cells divide in order to multiply and form beings. In this context, I am not sure division is even the right term to use, since in this process nothing is lost or damaged. Rather, there is increase, and then the formation of a synthesis when all the pieces come together in splendid harmony. Everything is uniquely formed, then perfectly copied to be doubled, quadrupled, and multiplied exponentially until a new being is fully formed. In the Creator's hands division is not a breaking apart of a larger whole but rather a multiplication to compose a far greater whole.

When talking about division, it is important to note that *division* and *difference* are not synonymous. It is possible to be different without being divided; it is also possible to be divided without being different. Humanity is immensely diverse, with innumerable differences in appearance, thought, and expression which change across time and geography. Taking time to ponder and celebrate differences is actually important in helping us understand and add to the larger composition. Not only can difference operate in unity, it can also improve unity.

Difference is not the problem; division and the desire to remain divided are. We do not have a complete picture of who we are when we are divided, and this lack of identity brings confusion, pain, and strife. Division pulls away where differences arise and sometimes even seeks to create differences where none exist in order to justify walls of exclusion and separation. These walled places are breeding grounds for fear, pride, and pain which should alert us to the fact that things are not as they should be.

What are these walled places? They can be physically visible lines, including geography, gender, race, and general physical appearance impacted by genes, disorders, socio-economic status, personal preferences, and time. They can be invisible lines such as thoughts and perspectives which are expressed in culture, philosophy, politics, and beliefs (religious or otherwise). We are divided across familial lines, between distant relatives, between siblings, between parents and children, and between spouses. We are even divided within ourselves—outwardly we may be one way, while inwardly something completely different. We find division at every level and in every aspect of the human experience.

Division first happened in the garden, when humankind chose to step away from the source of life, and we were thus first introduced to pain, something to alert us that things are not okay. Understandably, we have a deep fear of pain, whether physical, emotional, or spiritual, and this fear drives us relentlessly to find solutions to try to escape pain by whatever means necessary. Sadly, this relentless pursuit to escape pain is generally independent of God (often even for those of us who know his voice) and so, our pursuit is just that: *our* pursuit. Outside of God's unifying standard, this pursuit has sadly only served to increase and multiply our fears. Fear of pain, shame, guilt, and death—the main driving forces behind division—are ironically also the fruits produced by it. Thus the cycle continues on and on until there is inevitable ruin, or until someone breaks free from the cycle.

The second voice that began speaking to humankind back in the garden, still speaks to us today. This serpent voice came to the first humans with a partial truth that directed them to break trust with the source of life to try to decide for themselves what was right and wrong. The second voice, the one later called the accuser, still speaks. He still tries to convince us that there is something worthwhile that exists apart from God, and from others. He still comes to us with partial truths and full lies that create or feed fear, shame, guilt, pride, rage, discouragement, envy, selfishness, immorality, idolatry, and a whole host of other destructive attitudes and behaviours. All these specifically target relationship and destroy unity. These are what divide nations, families, and souls. The second voice is bent on dismantling and destroying the beautiful whole that God has designed and desired from the start. Every difference designed by the Creator has the potential to enrich, strengthen, or beautify the whole, but if seen through the false lens offered by the second voice, difference is instead rejected, exploited, mocked, altered, or wiped clean out.

When I was a child, during many Christmas vacations the whole family would be engaged in piecing together a large jig-saw puzzle. It would take many days and call upon the different skill sets of each family member to construct the puzzle. My dad would sort and group colours and patterns. My brother would persistently and patiently try pieces in various spots until they worked. My mother would encourage us all, and I loved trying to troubleshoot pieces that we simply could not seem to place anywhere. I would examine the piece carefully in reference to the picture on the puzzle box until I could determine exactly where that particular piece needed to be placed. The picture on the puzzle box was a lifeline. None of the pieces made any sense outside of the picture they were designed to form.

A puzzle piece on its own separate from the others is tiny, insignificant, uninteresting, and out of place. Imagine if I took one of those pieces out of the puzzle box and tried to make it stand out. Maybe by beautifully framing it and hanging it on a wall. Maybe by claiming it was in the shape of, or signed by, or owned by some famous celebrity, and then placing a huge price tag on it. Maybe by claiming it had been prayed over by a famous holy man and carried special powers. Maybe by destroying the rest of the puzzle pieces so that it would be the only one, and thus stand out. Maybe by claiming it contained a secret scandalous image of someone, and then trying to use it as blackmail. There are a multitude of ridiculous things I could do to try to draw attention to one tiny piece of a puzzle, to try to give it more value. But the fact is, it would remain nothing more than a puzzle piece. And, while a puzzle piece is actually quite beautiful—no two pieces in a puzzle are exactly alike, and each piece is so uniquely formed that no other piece can fit where it has been designed to fit—what gives a puzzle piece its beauty and uniqueness can only be understood in relation to all the other pieces. That puzzle piece has a specific purpose and a specific place, and outside of that, it has no meaning or value.

Alone, a puzzle piece is barely noticeable, but when it is missing from the puzzle to which it belongs, its absence is keenly felt. You can find news stories about people who have worked for months on a massive jigsaw puzzle only to discover a piece missing. On its own, a puzzle piece is nothing, but in a completed puzzle, it is everything.

While the second voice, the voice of the accuser, continues to speak to us, trying to rip apart the beautiful puzzle that has been designed and is currently being constructed, the first voice also continues to speak to us. The first voice is the voice of the Creator who spoke all that is into being: the voice of life. The first voice is the voice of the good shepherd, the voice of love. He spoke the first word and he also has the last word. His voice offers a response to every one of the second voice's attempts to destroy the beautiful whole that God desires and is fashioning. God's voice continually calls us back to him, for he is the standard which binds and holds all things together. His voice comes to us with truth, love, honour, humility, pardon, peace, encouragement, joy, selflessness, purity, covenant, and a whole host of other life-giving attributes. He gives meaning and beauty to all that is, for he is life. He does not have to respond to the second voice, or to ours, but he does, because he is good and because he is writing the story.

In the face of the broken state of his creation, God makes provision for humanity to be able to survive and thrive to the end of this current story. His provision is often not what we, the created, expect or imagine. Nor is it often what we understand, or necessarily prefer. As such, our tendency is to pull away or even flat out reject his provision. Yet it is there, always there. This story that we find ourselves in is the story of a perfectly good God who grants to us "all things that pertain to life and godliness."[3] It is the story of provision even for those who have chosen to live in a state of division. It explains God's provision for us, not only to escape this state, but also to live whole and unified, while still being a work in progress.

Because of God's provision, every moment is pregnant with opportunity. Opportunity to listen to the first and not to the second voice. Opportunity to choose to accept God's standard, and so choose wholeness and life. Or to continue deciding for ourselves without reference to him, and so continue in brokenness and eventual ruin. Opportunity has been there right from the start. In the garden the first man and woman were presented with two scenarios: the tree of life versus the tree of the knowledge of good and evil. After being expelled from the garden, the first generation of humankind, Cain and Abel, were also presented with the option to do good and be accepted, or to not do good and face the consequences. Each following generation was also presented with the same options; but we read that those who listen and respond to the first voice instead of the second are few and far between.

In the sixth chapter of Genesis we come to perhaps one of the most shocking and heartbreaking points in this story. God

[3] 2 Peter 1:3

is actually grieved that he has created humankind. What was supposed to be the pinnacle of his creation, what was meant to display and demonstrate his core nature, which is to experience and demonstrate love, was doing just the opposite, and continuously. "The LORD saw that the wickedness of man was great in the earth...every intention of the thoughts of his heart was only evil continually."[4]

Over and over again, humankind had chosen to do what was right in their own eyes without regard for the Creator or for one another. They had inherited and had also chosen disconnection and pain, and had forced the earth to suffer along with them. We read that God, "determined to make an end of all flesh, for the earth [was] filled with violence *through* them."[5] By refusing God's standard, by refusing connection with the source of life, humankind had chosen ruin for themselves, and for all that had been given into their care.

We know from the story that God did not design humankind for evil or to be evil; he made them for good and to be good. He gave them the capacity to live and reign well by giving them access to all that they needed and could possibly ever want, but with the freedom to choose. From the story we also know that, even when humanity did not choose God and his standard for good, God held onto hope that because they *could*, some of them still *would*. He hoped and believed that some would yet learn to love and be loved, that some would still reign well, even if only a few. We read that "creation was subjected to futility, not willingly, but because of him who subjected it, *in hope* that the creation itself [would] be set free from

---

[4] Genesis 6:5
[5] Genesis 6:13 italics mine

its bondage to corruption and obtain the freedom of the glory of the children of God."[6] Those who listen and respond to the first voice not only experience life and love, they spread it to others and to all that they have been given to care for. They live in freedom and reign well.

Even in the dire conditions preceding the flood, we read that God still made provision for humanity, for he still had hope. God offered a temporal escape from the ruin that has been embraced by humankind. He found one man who had chosen connection and surrender, and gave him instructions. God let Noah know where all flesh was heading and what needed to be done in order to escape that destruction. Noah listened, responded, and warned others. Through one man who was still listening to the first voice, God was able to let humanity know that, while their current path was destruction, if they would listen and accept his provision, then they could yet live.

God gave humanity plenty of time to consider their options. Noah was presumably building that large vessel for decades, ample time for people to choose a different path, to choose surrender, to choose life. In the story we read that, "God waited patiently in the days of Noah while the ark was being built..."[7] He was waiting for more to respond. I am convinced that had there been others besides Noah and his family who trusted the warning voice, who believed the choice for life was not as they understood or perhaps wanted, then they, too, would have been taken into the ark and saved. But as we know, "only a few people, eight in all, were saved through water."[8]

[6] Romans 8:20-21 italics mine
[7] 1 Peter 3:20 NIV
[8] Ibid.

After the flood, the problem of humankind choosing the wrong tree to eat from and the wrong

voice to listen to continued. The people gathered in the land of Shinar and purposed to build a tower that would reach to the heavens. Their reasoning was to make a name for themselves so as to avoid being scattered across the earth. Their motivation demonstrated that they, too, had listened to the second voice inviting them to decide for themselves what was good and right, instead of listening to the first voice which had called them to "fill the earth and subdue it".[9] This was an act of worship to the god of their own creation and a kingdom of their own making. But God intervened by confusing their language, which encouraged and essentially forced their dispersal across the earth.[10]

Even as the tribes began to speak in different languages, and so were scattered to different lands, God still sought a people who would listen and respond to his voice as his means to speak to all of humanity. He chose one listening man, Abram, and declared that he would establish a nation through his line, that through him "all the families of the earth shall be blessed".[11] God's plan was that this nation, to be given the name Israel, was to be an ongoing, visible example for all humankind of what relationship with the Creator looks like. A phrase that is repeated in various places in the stories about Israel is: *that they may know that I am the LORD.* All that God does with respect to humankind is that they may know him. He knows that life is entirely dependent upon and bound up in him,

---

[9] Genesis 1:28
[10] Genesis 11:4-9
[11] Genesis 12:3

and so God continuously invites humankind to know him as the great 'I am', to come to him to find life. God established Israel to demonstrate to all flesh what surrender to him looks like, but also what separation from him looks like.

Abram was later given the name Abraham, 'father of many', and the generations after him were indeed many. They grew into a vast nation which was given the name Israel, 'struggles with God'. Such an appropriate description of the relationship between the Creator and humankind! God's favour upon the nation of Israel sparked fear in the people of the land they came to dwell in. The Egyptians became afraid, "the people of Israel are too many and too mighty for us...let us deal shrewdly with them, lest they multiply, and, if war breaks out, they join our enemies and fight against us and escape from the land."[12] The Egyptians decided that the solution to this fear was to weaken the people of Israel by making them slaves, and by seeking to kill every male born to them. After a few centuries of this 'shrewd' treatment, Israel, who was in unique relationship with the Creator, had been crying out to him. Israel's voice was heard, and God responded in the fullness of time with one of the most elaborate stories of provision we have yet seen in this story; it serves as a foreshadow of what is to come much later on. In the story of Israel's exodus from the land of Egypt. God put on display for all humanity that listening and responding to his voice (whether they are Israelites or not) will bring life and freedom, whereas refusing him—deciding for themselves what is good—results in ruin and destruction.

---

[12] Exodus 1:9-10

Every time the Pharaoh believed Moses and Aaron and what they spoke on behalf of God, he and his people were released from judgments issued against them. Conversely, every time the Pharaoh rejected the warnings of Moses and Aaron and returned to following his own ideas and those of his advisors, he and his nation suffered with increasing intensity. In the midst of the turmoil, we read that God continuously gave instructions on how to avoid destruction. God's word through Moses and Aaron included pre-plague warnings as well as instructions about how to be saved in the midst of some of the plagues, such as bringing people and livestock indoors during the hail. But the final instruction was for the children of Israel alone: placing the blood of lambs upon the doorposts of every house to protect them when the angel of death would come. As the Israelites were finally released to leave, "many other people went up with them,"[13] so, among the Egyptians, there were also those who heard and responded to the voice of God and were saved along with the Israelites.

After an unbelievable showdown of warnings, refusals, and increasingly harsh judgments, Israel was finally released from the Pharaoh's control and headed into the wilderness to worship. Moses, standing before the newly freed nation, who had just seen so clearly what surrender to God's voice versus rebelling against it brings, must still present to them the same choice that was offered back in the garden. Moses extended the same choice that God has been continually offering to each and every generation of humankind. "I have set before you today life and goodness, as well as death and disaster...love the

---

[13] Exodus 12:38 NIV

LORD your God...walk in His ways, and...keep His command-
ments, statutes, and ordinances, so that you may live and increase."[14]

The relationship between God and the nation of Israel continued on in the story. This unique relationship continued to be
God's primary vehicle for communicating with all of humankind, and so he spoke regularly to Israel about his provision
and about the way to life. Sadly, we read that this nation regularly rebelled against Moses' leadership, and thus rebelled
against God. Very few chose to submit to God's standard; yet
God continually sought out those who would listen and respond and, thankfully, there are those who did. Multiple prophets were sent by God to communicate what they received directly to the nation of Israel, and indirectly to the nations of the
world. The details may vary but the core message is the same,
which is well summarized in this word from the prophet Amos:

Seek the LORD and live...you who turn justice to
wormwood and cast down righteousness to the
earth! He who made the Pleiades and Orion, and
turns deep darkness into the morning and darkens
the day into night, who calls for the waters of the
sea and pours them out on the surface of the earth,
the LORD is his name...Seek good, and not evil,
that you may live; and so the LORD, the God of
hosts, will be with you...[15]

[14] Deuteronomy 30:15-16 BSB
[15] Amos 5:6-8,14

The One who made the stars, who made the day and the night, who pours forth rain, who can and has flooded the earth, who scattered the peoples, who chose a nation to display his relationship with humankind, the One who designed all that is, his name is 'I am'. He has heavenly hosts at his disposal. He is sovereign, He knows what he is doing. He knows what is good, because he is good. He says to all those who cast righteousness down by choosing to live by their own standards, seek him and you *will* find life, seek him and he *will* be with you.

4

We'll Enter In As The Wedding Bells Ring

"Have you thought of an ending?"
"Yes, several, and all are dark and unpleasant."
"Oh, that won't do! Books ought to have good endings. How
would this do: and they all settled down and lived together
happily ever after?"
"It will do well, if it ever came to that."
"Ah! And where will they live? That's what I often wonder."
—J.R.R. Tolkien[1]

He and I, in that bright glory,
One deep joy shall share—
Mine, to be forever with Him;
His, that I am there.
—Gerhard Tersteegen[2]

[1] Tolkien, J.R.R. *The Fellowship of the Ring.* New York: Houghton Mifflin Company, 1994.
[2] Tozer, A W. *The Christian Book of Mystical Verse.* Christian Publications, Inc., 1963.

G od has been saying right from the beginning to humanity caught up in division and on a path to destruction that we should come to him and live. He has been, is, and will be all that we ever need. He has made provision for life, which ultimately means provision for unity. God has made it possible for humanity to be reconciled and united with him, and in turn for them to be reconciled and united with one another.

Provision for unity is one of a number of central themes in our story. I have chosen this particular theme as a primary lens through which to look at the works of God because of what the word 'provision' carries. The word 'provide' comes from the Latin *providere,* which means 'to foresee' or 'attend to' and so there is a sense of preparation involved in anticipation of a new circumstance. You make provision to prepare for planned events, but also when things do not go as planned. For example, you set aside provisions for a long journey, or you lay up provisions for a famine or some other potential catastrophe. Provision is there to help us get through planned or unplanned, unpredictable, or undesirable circumstances. Provision is a means to an end, an essential piece in the equation; but not the final piece, not the end goal. Provision makes a final destination or result attainable or reachable. God makes provision for humankind so that we can make it to the final pages of this story, prepared and ready. All of his provision is there to carry us along the journey towards denouement and it is also there to set the stage for the final chapter in this story we are in.

We therefore need to understand where we are heading and what we are facing in order to fully understand what we need to be prepared. God's provision will only make sense in this context. Though the final chapter has yet to be fully delivered because it has yet to be lived, we do know a little of what is going to happen. The culmination of our story involves a few different metaphorical pictures.

First of all, we are told that our current story ends with a wedding party—a joyful celebratory feast at the marriage of the Lamb to the bride, which is the marriage of the Son to the church.[3] The story culminates in the long promised, long desired new covenantal union finally being realized. A wedding symbolizes desired, mutual, and total commitment. The end is not about some simple superficial union, not some fling for a season, nor is it just about some big, one-time party. No, the end of the current story involves humankind entering a new family—entering and *committing to* that new family for all eternity. It is a beautiful and sobering metaphor. Wedding vows are not to be taken lightly. When two people enter into a marital union, they become something new, they become one, a greater whole than what either was as an individual. The Son takes great pains to woo the bride and prove the glory of his family. The chosen bride in turn takes great pains to keep herself pure and to keep her eyes focused on her bridegroom.

Secondly, we are told that the story ends with a new Jerusalem coming down out of heaven. Like the wedding feast, Jerusalem is a significant metaphor to include in the finale. In this story that we find ourselves in, Jerusalem is the city which represents the meeting place between God and humankind.

> Then I saw a new heaven and a new earth, for the
> first heaven and the first earth had passed away,
> and the sea was no more. And I saw the holy city,

[3] Revelation 19:7

new Jerusalem, coming down out of heaven from God, prepared as a bride adorned for her husband. And I heard a loud voice from the throne saying, "Behold, the dwelling place of God is with man. He will dwell with them, and they will be his people and God himself will be with them as their God."[4]

In the unique relationship established between the Creator and Israel, Jerusalem is the city where the temple was placed. The temple was the more permanent structure of the tabernacle, which was the place where Moses would regularly listen and respond to God while in the desert with the newly freed people of Israel. Long, detailed instructions were given to Moses about the construction of the tabernacle. In this tent of meeting was found the mercy seat, the place where Moses would hear God's voice speak to him. The mercy seat was later moved to the temple, into the holy of holies, where the consecrated high priest would go to meet with God once a year on behalf of the nation. The temple in Jerusalem was the place where humankind (both Jews and Gentiles) could, because of mercy, come to pray to God, and it was where God would listen to them.[5] It was the place where humankind could come to make things right with God according to his standard through the appointed and anointed priesthood.[6]

The temple was a copy, a representation of a heavenly reality. It was a bridge of connection between heaven and earth,

---

[4] Revelation 21:1-3
[5] 2 Chronicles 6:18-7:3, 12-16
[6] 1 Kings 8:27-30; 9:3

mercy extended between the perfect world of the Godhead and our divided broken world. To speak of a new Jerusalem therefore, is to speak of a new meeting place for the Godhead and humankind, and a new dwelling place for both of them.

The new Jerusalem comes down from above. It is spiritual and eternal, not earthly and temporal, like the former Jerusalem. A new Jerusalem is the place where the covenantal marriage vows that were continuously broken and defiled in the demonstrative relationship between God and Israel in the early parts of the story can finally be renewed with sincerity, and actually fulfilled. We are told that the current story will end with God now having his permanent dwelling place with humankind,[7] with those he has called through his mercy, who have responded by believing and choosing the Son, who desire to be married to him, to be in the family of God. This current story will end with no more division, no more separation, but with an incredible new eternal family in their eternal home.

Finally, we are also told that the current story ends with the restoration of God's original plan for creation, specifically, for humankind. We read that in the last chapter of the story, a new humankind (one born of spirit, not of flesh) will have the right of full access to the tree of life,[8] a right which had been removed back in the garden when the first man and woman ate from the tree of the knowledge of good and evil instead of the tree of life. We are told that in the final chapter, the new humankind will no longer be living in a state of perpetual division but rather in a state of total and complete unity. They will fi-

[7] Revelation 21:3
[8] Revelation 22:14

nally accept God's standard of good, no longer trying to establish and walk according to their own standard. We are told that this humankind will live in this state forever as they partake of the tree of life.

These beautiful pictures are promised to those who believe. The One who is writing this story continually reveals to us that this is the ending he wants humankind to arrive at.

However, we are told about another piece to come in the final chapter, a piece which is deeply distressing and frightening, but also completely necessary and just. At the end of our current story we find the pronouncement of judgment, the formal and final decision concerning just punishment. We are told that at the end of this story come the final scenes of the suffering, pain, and loss that have been present and continuing in intensity and frequency since the very beginning.

The judgment piece, which includes violence, plagues, and natural disasters, can come across as harsh and confusing to our limited sensibilities about what is good or bad. Yet we also cry out in anger when perpetrators of evil are not held accountable and punished for their crimes. God's judgment is simultaneously feared and desired. The judgment piece is linked with, and is, in fact, inseparable from the promised picture of complete eternal unity. There simply cannot be a perfect, eternal union without a total and final breaking off of all that is evil. There must be a final destruction of all that has been causing division throughout the story, that has chosen the created over the Creator, that refuses to come under God's unifying standard of good.

We are heading towards a new unified family through marriage with the Son in the Godhead, and towards a new Jerusalem where this family can live together for all eternity. We are also heading towards a final judgment. Judgment is not something that is suddenly introduced at the end of this story; it is present right from the beginning and a recurring theme throughout.

Back in the garden, after God has explained the consequences of humankind choosing to eat from the wrong tree, and after he has made the first provision for humankind, covering their shame, God makes an interesting statement. He says, "Behold, the man has become like one of us in knowing good and evil."[9] God is saying that humans now know more than his good standard; they now know what it is to be outside of this standard, to be outside of him. They now know evil. God's response to this circumstance is to immediately block their access to the tree of life. Because humankind has accepted a separate standard and has ushered in division, they have brought judgment upon themselves which is the judgment of the "prince of this world."[10] That judgment is this: what is separate from God—the source of life—should not, and indeed cannot remain forever. We cannot go on eternally rebellious, eternally separate from the Creator and sustainer of all things. Thinking we are wisely deciding for ourselves our own standard, we have actually entered a kingdom of darkness. We have come under the authority of the prince of this world, the prince of flesh, whose kingdom is not eternal and whose end is destruction. He is contrary to God, and thus contrary to light and

[9] Genesis 3:22
[10] John 12:31

life. We must surrender to the Creator's one standard or remain in darkness and nothingness outside of it.

To get to the promised ending of a beautiful unity, humanity needs a way to escape or overturn the final ruling concerning us. We need to know the way to make it through just judgment. We then need to learn how to become a worthy, beautiful bride for the marriage. We need to know our part in making ready the place for our eternal dwelling. God's provision, all of it, serves these purposes. In the next chapter we will look in more detail at God's most central and profound provision for humanity to be made clean, to be made new that they may be set free from eternal punishment.

5

There is Power in the Blood

*You can't live without blood. So it's a very symbol of life.
Now, the altar is a symbol of God, and the people are gathered there before it. Moses takes the blood and sprinkles
some of it on the people, and then some on the altar, to show
that they are united, God and the people. There is a bond of
that gift of life, symbolized by blood. They share God's life.
God shares their life later in Jesus. So it's a sign of the covenant...God's life is shared with the people, symbolized by that
blood.*
—Thomas Gumbleton[1]

*The Lord's Supper is a token, not only of union with Jesus,
but of union with all His people. The visible Church of God is
split up into sects and parties known by the names of men; it
can hardly be looked upon by men as one Church, and yet in
God's sight it is one, and never can be anything else than one.*

---

[1] "Our Covenant Unites Us with God and with One Another." *National Catholic Reporter*, 14 June 2012, www.ncronline.org/blogs/peace-pulpit/our-covenant-unites-us-god-and-one-another.

In this highest act of worship, coming round the Lord's table, in one place or in another—church, chapel, room, mountain side, or dungeon—you acknowledge this truth, that you are one in the blood of the Lamb with every child of God.
—Steven A. Blackwood

The Triune God dwells in unity and his desire for and from his creation is the same: unity. From the moment that humankind chose the flesh, chose the created over him, from the moment that we became divided and separated from life, God has made provision for unity to still be possible. Clearly the selfish, destructive behaviours of humankind are obstacles to connection and unity, and these need to be controlled; but therein lies the difficulty. How is an independent, selfish will to be controlled so that it does not harm itself or another, while still allowing it the freedom and capacity to choose love?

Let's first understand a bit better the crux of the problem for which we need provision. There is a metaphor found in the physical realm which I believe offers a visual representation of the nature and severity of sin—which is trying to establish a standard for what is good outside of the Creator. In this story that we find ourselves in, sin and disease are frequently spoken of and addressed simultaneously. We see this when the Psalmist declares that God "forgives all your sins and heals all your diseases"[2] or when Jesus first forgives a man's sins and then also heals his paralyzed body.[3] There is a link between sin and disease; something can therefore be learned about the one by looking at the other.

[2] Psalm 103:3 NIV
[3] Mark 2:1-12

Considering disease and, quite specifically, the disease of cancer, we find a physical metaphor for the spiritual reality of sin. The term 'cancer' covers a wide variety of devastating conditions that develop over time and touch every segment of humanity. Cancer is not like most diseases; it is not some virus or bacteria that comes from outside to invade the body, it begins *in* the body, almost anywhere. While there are things in the environment which are linked with causing cancer (carcinogens), they do not cause cancer at all times and under all circumstances, nor can or should they necessarily be avoided at all costs.[4] Carcinogens are things which can cause cancer but *they* are not cancer. Cancer is the uncontrolled growth of abnormal cells which happens when the body's normal control mechanism stops working. Cancer cells are essentially cells that have stepped outside of their original purpose and their normal, expected behaviour. They are cells which now have no role, no valid place in the body, and yet increase exponentially. Cancer begins when a cell breaks free from the normal restraints on cell division and begins to follow its own agenda for proliferation. Cancer kills when these abnormal cells invade key organs and interfere with the body functions necessary to live.[5] Similarly, sin begins when the created breaks free from the normal restraints on division and begins to follow its own agenda. Sin destroys when it invades and interferes with the healthy functions of individual souls and the larger whole.

---

[4] "Known and Probable Human Carcinogens." *American Cancer Society*, www.cancer.org/cancer/cancer-causes/general-info/known-and-probable-human-carcinogens.html.

[5] (US), National Institutes of Health. "Understanding Cancer." *NIH Curriculum Supplement Series [Internet].*, U.S. National Library of Medicine, 1 Jan. 1970, www.ncbi.nlm.nih.gov/books/NBK20362/.

It is important to note that, when cancer destroys a body, it also destroys itself. When there are no longer any healthy cells to keep the body going, the cancer has no way to be nourished, and so cannot live either. When humans become set on deciding for themselves what is good and what is evil, when what they do benefits them alone to the detriment of others, when their desires and behaviours cease to benefit the greater whole, then they lose their original purpose and place in that greater whole. It is only a matter of time before what is healthy will be compromised and the greater whole will no longer be able to function. As with cancer, the result of sin is a slow, painful ruin. James warns us that "sin when it is fully grown brings forth death."[6]

A will, which is unwilling to accept the standard of good established by the Creator, the source of life, is behaving abnormally. Such a will tends to take more than it gives, tends to look after itself without regard for the larger whole, and tends to flourish at the expense of others. Such a will can actually have no part in another; it cannot truly know love, because love desires and seeks the good of another, not its own. "To love (which is to live) is to be seeking, fostering, and sustaining connections with that which is different and other—without domination, absorption, or fusion—in delight, in care, in compassion."[7] To forcefully, grudgingly, or selfishly take, while rejecting what is given, is not love. Love willingly, joyfully, and sacrificially gives, and freely receives what is given.

---

[6] James 1:15
[7] Olthuis, James H. *The Beautiful Risk: a New Psychology of Loving and Being Loved.* Wipf & Stock, 2006.

To love is to be patient and kind when another grieves, not to envy but rather be glad for and with another. To love is not to boast but rather to exalt others, not to demand but to be grateful for praise. To love is not to control but rather to submit. To love is not to defend but rather to confess. To love is not to blame but instead to forgive. To love is not to divide but to seek to reconcile. To love is to woo, to commit, to bond, and to remain. As the Trinity, God is an everlasting, divine community of perfect submission, perfect joy, and perfect covenant with himself. Humankind was created to enter this divine community. This is *normal*. Humankind's rejection of the loving community of the Trinity is abnormal.

What is preventing humankind from arriving at the desired conclusion to this current story—perfect unity—is that which is abnormal, meaning everything which is contrary to unity. Any attitude, thought, or behaviour opposed to the one standard in which all can be held together, divides and ultimately destroys us. Just as the Father was in him, and he was in the Father, Jesus prayed that all those who believe in him will also be in them.[8] But in order for humankind to enter the divine community, they must be of a new nature,[9] and of a different will,[10] one that is surrendered fully to the will of the Godhead. But humankind became collectively contrary to God's will because they became contrary to his standard; all are in an abnormal, un-surrendered state. The solution is to get rid of the abnormal. In this state we will, and indeed must die. God's pronounced judgment is a necessary and final decision.

[8] John 17:21, 23
[9] John 3:5-6; 2 Peter 1:4
[10] Luke 22:42

If we consider a will outside of God's will to be like cancer—something abnormal, having forgotten its original design and purpose, something trying to take for itself, and not allowing the head of the body to determine its place and its boundaries—then perhaps we can better understand God's judgment. Like cancer, sin must be eradicated or it will only increase, destroying others until it has also completely destroyed itself.

A phrase we frequently see early in the story is a directive to *purge the evil from among you.* This is essentially a command to destroy cancerous cells. Yet, just as an expert doctor is needed to decide which cells should be destroyed and how, likewise God must be the one to determine what must be purged and how. Ideally, cancer is removed without destroying any healthy parts along with it; yet often the healthy must be taken out along with the cancer since there is no simple way to separate the two. This is what makes cancer so horrific, and also what makes sin so horrific. The crux of humanity's difficulty is that the cancer of sin is intertwined with our persons; it is in our minds, emotions, and bodies; it is in our wills. The only way to remove all trace of it, really, is to die. God's righteousness and necessary judgment, the solution to rid humankind of the cancer of sin, is actually what stands in the way of all of us making it to the final chapter of this story.

God's greatest provision for humankind then is specifically connected to his final judgment. His greatest provision is actually death. God's provision for unity to still be possible is destruction of all that which has stepped outside of its original purpose, all that which has ceased to obey the head or contribute to the whole. Death is God's means to rightly destroy that which causes pain and destruction. There must be a complete purification. Death is necessary. Through the purification process that God has provided, humankind has a way to pass through the all consuming fire of judgment without being completely destroyed along with the cancer of sin.

This story we are in speaks a great deal about blood. Blood is another of the physical metaphors given to help us understand a deeper reality. We are told that blood represents life, specifically the life of all flesh. Blood carries what is needed to each of the organs in a body in order for them to function. Blood must be clean; it must be full; and it must move. Pour out the blood, and life is poured out. God tells humankind that they are not to consume meat with the blood, whether meat caught on a hunt,[11] domestically prepared,[12] or offered as sacrifice.[13] We are told that blood has been given to humankind as atonement on God's altar.[14] Blood on the altar represents justice, a covering over or a pacifying of wrath over life *taken* through life *given*. To offer blood on the altar is to offer life up to God, to willingly give back what he has given. It is an act of surrender and obedience.

The purpose of a blood sacrifice is atonement. This English word 'atonement' was actually created[15] to describe what is happening in this process. Rooted in a Latin word for unity, atonement is about reconciling or restoring harmony; it quite literally means at-one-ment. When we choose to surrender, when we choose not to do what is right in our own eyes but

[11] Leviticus 17:13
[12] Deuteronomy 12:15-16
[13] Deuteronomy 12:27
[14] Leviticus 17:11 GNT "The life of every living thing is in the blood, and that is why the Lord has commanded that all blood be poured out on the altar to take away the people's sins. Blood, which is life, takes away sins."
[15] First used in William Tyndale's English translation of scripture.

instead listen to the voice of the Creator, then we choose to be 'at one'.

In the former covenant between God and humankind, specifically between God and the chosen nation of Israel, we read of God's expectations from people, his promises to them, and his provision for them. One thing we read in this covenant is that they were not to partake of blood, only to offer it up to God. The solution to sin committed by the people was sacrifice, and frequently a blood sacrifice because the answer to selfish rebellion is willing surrender. The blood sacrifice was a symbolic representation of a deeper unseen reality, a copy of what was happening in the spiritual realm, and a picture of what was to come. The blood of animal sacrifice does not fully benefit us since they, like us, are flesh. The animal sacrifices were "but a shadow of the good things to come instead of the true form of these realities...in these sacrifices there [was] a reminder of sins."[16] Animal sacrifice was a very graphic demonstration and continuous reminder of the cost of sin, the consequences of a will divided. To offer a life up on the altar to God was an act of surrender. It was listening and responding to the first voice; it was acknowledging the severity of the problem and recognizing the great cost of the problem which is the life of a pure, blemish free, guiltless creature.

God's temporary, symbolic answer to the problem of sin was to give animals, but his ultimate answer was to give of himself, to give of the divine trio. The Son is given by the Father, but he also volunteers and willingly gives himself. Jesus is the provision for the final judgment. Jesus takes on flesh; he takes on our state of abnormality, but is not altered by it. Jesus

[16] Hebrews 10:1, 3

is the only one who can endure the horrific process of removing all the cancer of sin and not be fully destroyed because *he* is healthy; *he* is pure. That which was to be destroyed in his death on the cross was taken upon Jesus, but none of it originated with him, all of it belonged to another. Jesus' will was not divided; it was fully surrendered. The death of Jesus was unique because it was given, not taken. It was a knowing, willing act of loving obedience. Incredibly, we are invited to partake of this.

Jesus' invitation to eat his flesh and drink his blood is both shocking and intensely profound. It is an invitation to partake of him, to be one with him. "Whoever feeds on my flesh and drinks my blood abides in me, and I in him."[17] His life was utterly clean as he passed through necessary and horrific judgment carrying the cancer of sin, so it was only sin that was destroyed, but he was raised to life. We read that Jesus is the firstborn of a new creation among many siblings.[18] When we partake of his blood (demonstrated and remembered by faith at the communion table), we take on his DNA as it were, as we become one with him in his death and his resurrection. We are born anew, "not of blood nor of the will of the flesh nor of the will of man, but of God."[19] We do not yet fully understand what this means exactly since we have not yet passed through final judgment into eternity. "We are God's children now, and what we will be has not yet appeared; but we know that when he appears we shall be like him, because we shall see him as he is."[20] Only the pure blood of Jesus can safely pass through

[17] John 6:56
[18] Romans 8:29
[19] John 1:13
[20] 1 John 3:2

judgment fire; without his blood we will be destroyed as we pass through. He takes our place in the judgment. He demonstrates perfect love by choosing to suffer just punishment in our place that we may have life.

Jesus is the standard of what it is to be fully and truly human; he is the second Adam. Jesus came to respond to the first and the second voice in the way that the first Adam should have responded. Adam listened to the second voice's invitation (through his wife) to forcefully take that which was already his—to be like God. When Jesus is offered a similar invitation by the second voice to forcefully take something that was already given to him—the authority and glory of all the kingdoms of the world—Jesus refuses. Adam hides from God's voice, saying he is afraid, but Jesus surrenders to it, saying "not my will, but yours be done."[21] Jesus came to show that being made in the image of God means to love the other more than self, to willingly give rather than take, to be vulnerable enough to receive from others, to trust and accede to the one standard for good rather than reject it by going one's own way.

Blood is not only a symbol of life; it is also a symbol of deep connection. We speak of blood ties as relationships of significance and of covenant. To partake of the blood of Jesus, which is a profound mystery, is an act of bonding and an act of commitment.[22] Through this blood bond with Jesus, we can access the Father and the Spirit; we have communion with the Godhead. Through the blood bond with Jesus, we begin to become something new even while still in this physical world. We begin to be a visible representation of an unseen reality. By

[21] Luke 22:42
[22] Hebrews 2:11

partaking of the blood, we are purified to be the temple of the Holy Spirit—the meeting place for God and humankind—and we become the body of Jesus in this world, going about doing and saying what he would do were he present. Israel's original mandate of demonstrating what relationship with the Creator can and should look like is brought to fulfilment through the blood of Jesus. The blood of the Son is the provision given by God to allow us to make it through the final judgment, to allow us to be reconciled to him.

When we are reconciled to him, we have access to him, to his life. Just as the Son was given and came to us, so, too, is the Spirit given and comes to us. The choice to receive the Son is a choice to receive the Spirit and be reconciled to the Father. A choice to listen to and respond to the Spirit leads us to receive the Son and return to the Father. The choice to listen to the Father is to recognize and receive the Son and the Spirit. The Bible records the Trinity's pursuit of and relationship with humankind. Throughout it we find God's voice speaking to us about who he is, what he expects, what he has done, what he will do, and how we may know him, know his voice.

In the next chapter we will consider in more detail the incredible provision of God's voice: how it has been and continues to be given to humankind, and the problems with how we have recognized or responded to his voice.

6

And He Walks With Me And He Talks With Me

*An obsession merely with doing all God commands
may be the very thing that rules out being the kind
of person that he calls us to be.*
—Dallas Willard[1]

*Genuine trust involves allowing another to matter and have
an impact in our lives. For that reason, many who hate and
do battle with God trust Him more deeply than those whose
complacent faith permits an abstract and motionless stance
before Him. Those who trust God most are those whose faith
permits them to risk wrestling with Him over the deepest
questions of life. Good hearts are captured in a divine wrestling match; fearful, doubting hearts stay clear of the mat.*
—Dan B. Allender[2]

[1] Willard, D. *Hearing God.* Downers Grove: InterVarsity Press; 2012.
[2] Allender, Dan B. *The Wounded Heart: Hope for Adult Victims of Childhood
Sexual Abuse.* Colorado Springs, CO: NavPress; 1995.

When we begin to read the Bible through the lens of provision, we can see it then through stories recorded as God's continuous giving to humankind. First he gives by creating them; then he gives by helping them understand who they are and the system within which they find themselves. He helps them to understand consequences of certain beliefs and behaviours versus the benefits and blessings of others. Ultimately, he gives by offering his perfect life—his blood—which is the way for them to pass safely through judgment. Underlying all of this provision is the incredible gift of his voice.

The Bible is a record of, and an invitation to humankind to continual conversation with the Creator. His voice comes to humankind through his Spirit (speaking directly or indirectly through prophets), through his Son, and through the written words of scripture. In the Bible we find that, if people come to him, or if they listen when he calls, then God meets them. In that meeting, God either tells them what needs to be done or shows something of himself in order to bring them back into alignment with the beautiful whole that he has designed and envisioned. In this chapter we will explore the interplay between God's voice and the Bible as we have it.

Equipped with the Bible as a faithful record of how God has spoken to humankind in the past, we feel prepared for the continuation of this story we find ourselves in. Indeed, it is a book that has been inspired and breathed to life by him for teaching, reproof, correction, and training, that we may be complete and equipped for every good work.[3] It is a record of essential laws and principles given to humankind for relating with God and with one another. And yet, the Bible is not an all

---

[3] 2 Timothy 3:16-17

encompassing rule book for how we are to think and behave in *every* situation that we will, or could ever face. That is simply not possible. To expect to have a complete list of do's and don'ts to tell us how to walk through every situation in life in every place is to completely miss why God would want to give laws and instructions in the first place. They are given to serve people, specifically, people in community. Laws and instructions, even the harsh ones, are provision for humanity to be able to live in healthy unity, with God and with one another. They give us a standard with boundaries, principles, expectations, and perspective, as well as judgments, to purge out that which destroys unity. God given laws and instructions recorded in print are provision for a creation deeply divided, and one that incessantly struggles to hear, recognize, and respond to his voice on a consistent basis.

The early laws given to humankind, mostly through Moses and for the nation of Israel, are like an initial guardian says Paul. They give us a glimpse into God's standard and reveal how far humankind has deviated from this standard, and thus reveal humankind's guilt. Paul actually says we are captive under this guardian until we, through faith, become free to accept God's standard. We are bound by law until we become mature sons, heirs of a promise, through faith.[4] Until we can fully interact with one another in perfect, continuous submission and lavish love like the Godhead, only then can we say with faith like Paul, that, "I have been crucified with Christ. It is no longer I who live, but Christ who lives in me."[5] Until we have

4 Galatians 3:19-4:7
5 Galatians 2:20

truly died to self, with Christ living in and through us, we need a just, unifying standard to help us—we need *his* standard.

His standard is and has always been given to us through the Spirit. The Spirit was upon Jesus who spoke to us of God's standard, and the Spirit inspired and breathed scripture, which is where much of this standard is recorded. In order to know God's standard in *any* and *every* circumstance, we still need his voice; we still need the Spirit. Through the blood of Jesus the Spirit is given to all who believe, and he speaks directly to us. Paul tells us that if we "walk by the Spirit...[we] will not gratify the desires of the flesh,"[6] for, "those who are led by the Spirit of God are the children of God."[7]

In this story that we find ourselves in, we read that when people listen and respond to God's voice, they encounter the source of all life. In that place of encounter, their hearts and their circumstances are brought to light so that they may see things as they are, and may find truth and freedom. In that place of encounter, sometimes God gives promises,[8] sometimes he gives responsibilities,[9] at times he reminds them of things he has spoken before;[10] at other times he gives seemingly new instructions;[11] and still at other times he simply meets them as a

---

[6] Galatians 5:16

[7] Romans 8:14 N IV

[8] Genesis 12:2, Exodus 6:1-8, 2 Samuel 7:8-16

[9] Jeremiah 1:4-11; Ezekiel 3:16-21

[10] For example Matthew 12:15-21; Luke 24:25-27; John 2:16-17; 5:46; 6:41-51; 12:37-41; with many more passages later in John which contain variations of the phrase 'in order that scripture might be fulfilled' (13:18, 15:25, 17:12, 18:9, 18:32, 19:24, 28, 36-37)

[11] For example, in Acts 10 we read that Peter has an encounter with God on the rooftop inviting him to do something which Jewish law strictly prohibited. If Peter had not had this vision, he would have missed that what Jesus had accomplished on the cross extended to all peoples. Another example is the very specific instructions by the Holy Spirit to "go to the street called Straight" (Acts 9:11) or forbidding them to preach in Asia (Acts 16:6)

friend.[12] As we now read these stories of encounter, we find principles which can be applied to our current circumstances; we find his standard. Yet even more than this, as we read these stories of encounter with the voice of God, we also find something revealed of our character, and of God's character. We get to know more of who we are, more of who he is, and more about the nature of all relationships.

The story of Job is a powerful and challenging, though unsettling example of an encounter with the voice of God. Job is described as a man who was blameless and upright, one who feared God and turned away from evil, and yet a day came when Job had lost all his children, his wealth, his dignity, and his health. But Job still blessed the LORD, "Naked I came from my mother's womb, and naked shall I return. The LORD gave, and the LORD has taken away; blessed be the name of the LORD."[13] His wife tried to provoke him to curse God, and his friends insisted he must have sinned terribly and so deserved what came, but Job wondered what was going on, and so sought the voice of God, convinced that in the end he would come forth as gold.[14]

Job and his friends seem to have a reasonable grasp of what God had thus far revealed to humankind in the story. The thoughts and principles Job and his friends speak about are fair and generally accurate based on what they have thus far seen and understood concerning humankind's relationship with their Creator, though they are certainly limited and biased. They have understood that listening to and obeying God brings

[12] Exodus 33:11
[13] Job 1:21
[14] Job 23:10

peace and blessing, while sin brings suffering and disaster. They have also understood that trying to defend one's own ideas about what is just or unjust before the Creator of the universe is futile; that submission and repentance bring peace, because judgment will find all of us in the end. The troubling part of this story is that these truths, which Job and his friends are using in order to analyze his situation, appear to be inconsistent with the circumstances before them, or at least they appear so to Job. Their understandings are not necessarily wrong but rather incomplete and misapplied when it comes to Job's experiences. There is some information that Job and his friends are not privy to.

The circumstances that confront Job and his friends are disturbing. Job's immense suffering bothers them greatly, not only because it is so extensive and so painful, but also because it seems to conflict with their understanding of the relationship between humankind and God. Unfortunately, neither Job nor his friends can see the total picture beyond the visible, tangible reality in front of them. They are forced to try to reconcile what they see with what they thus far know, not fully aware that more light is needed in order to properly assess the situation.

The response of Job's friends to this seeming clash is to try to make Job's circumstances fit their understanding, and they work very hard at trying to convince him that his suffering is due to his sin. Job's friends have not been speaking *to* God, they have been speaking *for* God, and even worse, they have even been implying that God does not speak. Zophar says to Job, "Oh, that God would speak and open his lips to you...can you find out the limit of the Almighty? It is higher than heaven—what can you do?"[15] Eliphaz declares that, "God puts no trust in his holy ones."[16] But as they begin to judge him as sinful and deserving of his present suffering, Job says to his friends, "What you know, I also know, but I would speak to the Almighty, and I desire to argue my case with God."[17]

So, while much of the dialogue is between Job and his friends as they react to one another, Job also goes directly to God with his frustration about his suffering and how it conflicts with what he understands of God and of himself. Job brings his painful and righteous confusion about what is happening to him directly before God to confront him about what he feels is unjust in his situation. Then, unlike his friends, Job expects, and waits for an answer from God.

And God does come, though the way he answers Job is perhaps unexpected. He responds by telling him all about some of the unique animals and processes found in nature. For the western reader especially, this response by God can seem odd, even disconcerting. The things that God speaks to Job about feel unconnected to anything that Job has been challenging God on, and certainly unrelated to Job's immense suffering. But if we look through a more eastern intuitive lens, we might recognize that here God is using figurative speech as a way to point Job to a deeper truth. God is talking about things which for Job, though familiar, are actually outside of his personal experience and far beyond his capacity to comprehend. No, Job was not there when the foundations of the earth were laid;[18] no, Job has

---

[15] Job 11:5, 7-8
[16] Job 15:15
[17] Job 13:3
[18] Job 38:4

never commanded the morning;[19] and no, Job has never walked in the recesses of the deep or had the gates of death revealed to him.[20] God speaks this way in order to indirectly and honourably lead Job to discover for himself that just as there are things in the world that are beyond his knowledge, wisdom, or experience, so, too, the circumstances of his life at the moment are beyond his capacity for understanding.

God does not ignore Job or remain silent: he sees and hears Job's cries; he shows up and meets with him. This, in and of itself, is an incredible honour and privilege. We find that there are so few people in the Bible who even want to, let alone are actually permitted to meet with God face to face. When God meets with Job, he does not rebuke Job for sinning, nor does he tell him he is wrong in his complaints. God shows up to indirectly let Job know that he has spoken the truth about God,[21] that his situation does *not* make sense, and that he is indeed experiencing unjust suffering.[22] But there are far bigger things at play than Job can grasp or enter into at this time.

In the story of Job, parallel to the drama taking place on earth, there is also a cosmic drama taking place in the unseen realm involving spiritual entities of good and evil. Our finite minds are given a glimpse into this unseen world of which we have little or almost no understanding. We, like Job's friends, will look at the circumstances in this story through our presently accepted standards about what is good or evil, and with

[19] Job 38:12
[20] Job 38:16-17
[21] Job 42:8
[22] While God does not say specifically to Job that his suffering was unjust, we understand this to be true since God presents Job to the accuser as blameless in chapter 1 and 2. Also, in Job 2:10 we read that in all the tragedy that had come upon Job he "did not sin with his lips."

our current understanding of who God is and how we think he should act. Even though we are given more insight into the story than Job and his friends, we, too, struggle to comprehend all that has happened to Job. Like Job and his friends, we, too, have a choice before us. We can either try to speak *for* God about what has happened in the story and use our human understanding to apply it to our current circumstances, or we can go directly *to* God and ask him to meet us in our confusion. We can ask him to help us understand the story as far as it is relevant to our particular situations. If we, like Job, can choose surrender and admit that there are things that are bigger than us at play, things greater than our present capacity to grasp, if we, like Job, can choose to trust God's character enough to say that there are "things too wonderful for me", then perhaps we, too, will believe that God can also meet us and give us as much understanding from Job's story as we need, and can presently handle. Perhaps we, too, will believe that God can meet us in whatever difficult circumstance we are currently in, to give us as much insight as we need to handle our challenge.

As I, too, have sat down with God to try to understand this story, I have found some pieces that I believe are relevant for us. In this story of Job, we usually see the central challenge as to the Creator of the universe and about his worthiness. The accuser claims that Job only listens to and obeys God's voice because of the benefits he receives, not because God is worthy to be obeyed. An accusation comes from the accuser and yet the original invitation to a challenge actually comes from God.

I believe the reason that this challenge over Job between God and the accuser is recorded here in our story is because it concerns something that humanity needs to understand about itself. It is something very relevant to us as it is to beings in the unseen realm, something that humanity has been created to reveal about the nature of God. The accuser's challenge calls into question a unique capacity that was given to humankind. He claims that humans only listen and respond to God's voice for selfish reasons (to get a blessing or to save oneself),[23] and so he charges that humans only fear God so long as it benefits them, subtly charging that they do not love him. The accuser implies that humans do not have the capacity to love without conditions attached, and that they now listen to the voice of the accuser, and his voice alone. The story of Job is relevant to all of us, for in it the accuser attempts to call into question our identity. He indirectly challenges the truth that humans are made in the image of God, with the capacity to think of the other, to love and to be loved. The accuser also questions the reality of our desire and ability to hear God's voice. The conclusion of Job proves that humankind can and still does choose to listen to God, and can indeed love in a covenantal way.

God does not fill Job in about the cosmic drama behind him because to do so would be to remove the central confusion altogether and thus remove the relevance of the accuser's claim and Job's response. God's response to Job's questioning about his suffering is something to the effect of:

Job, I hear you, I see and know your suffering, and that is why I have come down to speak with you. I am here. You rightly recognize that in this situation, while it is the enemy who has attacked you, it is I who have allowed it. You also rightly assess that you are undeserving. What you do not understand yet is

---

[23] Job 1:9-11; 2:4-5

that you are part of something so much greater than your temporal life here. Your life belongs to all of humanity, and through this situation, your life will speak for and to all of humanity, and in fact to all of creation. Right now, I cannot explain to you all the details of this drama, but these details are a key piece in the bigger story that you are in. But Job, even though you don't know all the details, you know me. You know that I am good and that you can trust me; so stay steady.

Of course, this response is my paraphrase with add-ins. God's answer is more cryptic, and I imagine many of us would prefer a fuller answer had we been in Job's place. But, interestingly, we must remember that God's answer is understood and received by Job, and he is completely satisfied with it. This cosmic drama and the conversations between the characters are clearly recorded for us to read and learn from, but we must not forget that the initial conversation happens between God and Job, not between God and Job's friends, and not between God and us. We may feel God's answer to Job is unsatisfying, yet the fact is Job agrees with it and finds it to be enough. Job says to God, "I know that you can do all things...I have uttered what I did not understand, things too wonderful for me, which I did not know...and [I] repent in dust and ashes."[24]

God honours and blesses Job for his attitude to his personal crisis, and for his response to God's answer to him in the midst of it. On the other hand, God rebukes Job's friends for their attitude and approach to Job's suffering. His friends do not come to God about this circumstance, and yet dare to speak into it about him, and for him. They pronounce judgment on their dear friend that is not only inaccurate, but also not theirs

[24] Job 42:2-3, 6

to pronounce. Yet, even with Job's friends, God has compassion. Though they do not come to him, God still comes to them. He reminds them of provision available to them, the provision of animal sacrifice. He also provides for them by inviting Job—who *is* seeking and listening to him—to pray on their behalf, that they may be released from judgment as a result of their unrighteous judgment upon another. God is so good.

The story of Job is evidence that the Bible is not a mere instruction manual on how to be a perfectly, healthy, whole human being, but more often a catalogue of stories. All of these serve as an invitation to converse with the God who inspired all of the stories, and who stars throughout them. In the story of encounter between God and Job, we find Job wrestling with his circumstances and engaging with God in his confusion and frustration. Here we see that humankind can expect and wait for an answer from God, and he will respond.

We find in the story of Habakkuk a similar situation of wrestling with circumstances and engaging with God about them. The prophet is deeply disturbed by the corruption and violence he sees in his nation and is wondering why God does not do anything about it. He declares, "I will take my stand at my watch-post and station myself on the tower, and look out to see what he will say to me..."[25] which is followed almost immediately with the words, "And the LORD answered me."[26] In scripture we find that we can wrestle and God will engage with us in that wrestling. Then God reveals to him that he will indeed do something about it by raising up another people group—a violent, bitter, and feared people group—to come

[25] Habakkuk 2:1
[26] Habakkuk 2:2

against the nation of Israel for just punishment. Habakkuk is then confused as to how or why God would choose to use such sinful people to execute justice upon his own people but his final response is similar to that of Job's, acceptance and trust.[27]

As we engage in conversation with God about the stories told in scripture—all the laws given, the mistakes made, the judgments, the blessings, the poetry, the laments, the proverbs, the revelations, and the prayers—we can learn how to live, really live. The Father in the divine community gives life and leads us to life, because he *is* life. He sends the Son and the Spirit as provision for that life. The Son in the divine community not only makes a way for us to come through judgment fire without being destroyed, he is also the example of a healthy and whole human being. The Spirit in the divine community reminds, teaches, comforts, reveals, guides, heals, and empowers us to be able to live as the Son lives, and draws us into perfect union with the Father, Son, and himself.

The priceless gift that we have been given in the Bible is essential for life. It clearly tells us the story of God's provision and points us to him and to his plan. But, just as we see from the story of Job, the Bible can be a difficult book to understand. In many places it proves to be challenging, mysterious, and, occasionally, even offensive. There are plenty of details we would love to find in the pages but which have clearly been left out, while some parts of the story feel arcane, and yet still other parts seem to conflict with, or contradict other parts of the story. What we must recognize is that the Bible was never meant to be a stand-alone book. It was given to us to supply

[27] Habakuk 3:17-18

and encourage connection with God; a record of the relationship between God and humankind that was never intended to replace that relationship. The more we examine this amazing story, the more we discover how uniquely and purposely it has been composed and organized. It is a book that actually demands conversation with its primary author in order to be fully understood and engaged with. Sometimes, like Job and Habakkuk, we hear directly from God as we bring questions up. Sometimes, God leads us to the right sources such as anointed teachers or books where we can find the answers. In other cases we may not have complete answers and will have to wait for more revelation. But in all our searchings, we know that God is pleased with our efforts and that he is a rewarder of those who diligently seek to find him.[28] At the same time, we must understand that not everything can be grasped by our finite minds at a particular time. Here is where we must trust implicitly in God's provision. For God's thoughts are higher than our thoughts and his ways are higher than our ways.[29]

In the next chapter we will look at the relationship we have with scripture and with God's voice in even more depth.

[28] Hebrews 11:6
[29] Isaiah 55:8

7

Ancient Words, Ever True

The revelation of a triune God in the unity of a single nature, the revelation of a divine Holy Spirit present in us, is not on the human level; it does not belong to the realm of reason. It is personal communication which God alone can give, and the task of giving it belongs to the Holy Spirit."
—Carlo Carretto[1]

The Bible is the written word of God, and because it is written it is confined and limited by the necessities of ink and paper and leather. The Voice of God, however, is alive and free as the sovereign God is free. "The words that I speak unto you, they are spirit, and they are life." The life is in the speaking words. God's word in the Bible can have power only because it corresponds to God's Word in the universe. It is the present Voice which makes the written word powerful.
—A. W. Tozer[2]

---

[1] Carretto, Carlo. *The God Who Comes*. Darton, Longman & Todd, 1974.
[2] Tozer A. *The Pursuit Of God*. La Vergne: Neeland Media LLC, 2017.

Each generation of humankind has had some access to a level of connection with God. The consistency, depth, or nature of that connection is not always the same, but it is always there. God makes provision for that to be possible. In this amazing story that we find ourselves in, connection with God seems to change or deepen over time as he enters the story, or writes or inspires new pieces of it. The new kinds of experiences or new levels of connection never negate, supersede, or replace the others; rather they confirm, fulfil, or expand upon them. God is ever communicating and engaging with humankind and the Bible is central and irreplaceable in this interaction. Scripture is not only a record of God's amazing provision for unity, but is itself also a means of provision for unity as it leads us to his standard and gives us boundaries within which to discern his voice and his provision.

We also observe though that possibly the greatest source of division in the people of God today centres around this book that we have been gifted with. How we interpret, understand, and apply it has led to division and brokenness, and even bloodshed for centuries. And so it is important to take some time to look deeper at how we, as part of the greater whole, can all together understand and interact with this incredible provision from God without devouring one another.

I live in a nation that is 99% Muslim and, as such, it is common to have conversations with friends and neighbours, shop-keepers and taxi drivers, or curious visitors to our church building about the differences between the Muslim and the Christian faiths. Often these discussions begin with comparisons of Muhammed with Jesus, or the Koran with the Bible. Such an approach initially makes sense since Muhammed and Jesus both lived among us, while the Koran and the Bible are both books. But at the foundation of this view is a misunderstanding that should, if possible, be addressed before trying to engage in more detail about where, how, and why our faiths differ. Understanding this underlying misconception is helpful in discussion with Muslims but it is also helpful for Christians in determining the place and role that the Bible has in our lives.

For both the Muslim and the Christian, revelation is that which comes down out of heaven to show humankind what they do not know. Revelation is to show God, who he is and what he expects for, and from, humankind. For both the Muslim and the Christian, God is so big and so mysterious, so *other*, that only *he* truly knows who he is. As such, only he can reveal, and accurately speak about himself. For the created to know him, God must tell them about himself. His voice and his words are the only way for humans to know him. For both the Muslim and the Christian, revelation of God comes as the word of God. The difference between these two faiths begins with how each recognizes and defines what is the word of God.

For the Muslim, the word of God is the Koran. The Koran—God's word—came down out of heaven and was dictated to Muhammed—perfect, complete, unalterable, and eternal. This understanding is why translations or updated Arabic versions of the Koran are not considered *the* Koran but only interpretations of it. It is why the Koran is approached with clean hands and body, why it is respected, kissed, and placed on the highest shelf in homes. It is why rules found in it which seem to belong to another time and culture are often expected to be obeyed exactly as they are. Since the Koran is the word of God for the Muslim, Muhammed is considered the messenger of

God. The Muslim believes that Muhammed is the one who heard, received, and recited the word of God, while others recorded it. Muhammed is one who recites the word of God.

For the Christian, however, God does not merely send a book, he ultimately reveals himself to humankind by having his word take on flesh.[3] Jesus is the living word of God. "Long ago, at many times and in many ways, God spoke to our fathers by the prophets, but in these last days he has spoken to us by his Son...[Jesus] is the radiance of the glory of God and the exact imprint of his nature."[4] The word of God is expressed through the beauty, complexity, depth, and mystery of a living, breathing, interacting human being. For the Christian, the Bible is a unique category of revelation. God not only came to earth as the living word, he also regularly communicated his message to humankind through human authors in and through their own unique cultures and contexts. It is an inspired document, not a dictated one. The written words in the Bible are inspired by the Spirit, and these testify to and record the living Word. The Bible is a different kind of revelation than Jesus. The Bible communicates the heart of the Godhead, but unlike Jesus, is not actually part of it. We do not worship God the Father, God the Son, and God the holy Bible. God's given words are beautiful, powerful, and necessary but it is with the Spirit, who communicates those words, and with the Son who is *the* word, that we have relationship. We do not have relationship with a written text.

[3] John 1:18
[4] Hebrews 1:1-3

Having such a perspective towards scripture in no way dismisses or downplays the Bible or its place in the life of a Christian. The Bible is essential and irreplaceable in our relationship with the Godhead. Understanding the difference between the nature of the living word versus the written text simply offers us necessary perspective when considering the purpose and role of the Bible in our lives in the here and now. Jesus said to the Jews who were persecuting him, "You search the scriptures because you think that in them you have eternal life; and it is they that bear witness about me, yet you refuse to come to me that you may have life."[5] The scriptures point us to life, but it is the living voice of God that gives life: "The hour is coming and has now come when the dead will hear the voice of the Son of God, and those who hear will live."[6]

As Christians, we love the Bible. We read, examine, study, analyze, and parse it; we meditate on and memorize it; we tell and we retell the stories we find in it; we live it. It tells us who we are, where we came from, where we are going, how we can get there, and what we can and must do along the way. We love it, because through it we are introduced to God. The more we get to know him, the more we find his voice in its pages; and the more we find his voice in the pages, the more we get to know him. It is a beautiful dance. We love the Bible because it continuously and increasingly leads us to him. It is the place of encounter with the Godhead and provides very necessary

---

[5] John 5:39-40
[6] John 5:25

boundaries for that relationship. But I wonder if in our enthu-
siasm for the Bible, we may go so far as to let it take the place
of real relationship with God himself.

Imagine with me a parable. Though it does not answer all
questions, it creates imagery to help us understand what it
looks like to interact with God and with scripture. A man and
a woman have recently become engaged. In the moments after
the proposal, the man sits the woman down in a lovely park
and then hands her a well-worn, lengthy journal. He smiles as
he explains that in her hands is a journal which his mother began keeping when she first learned she was pregnant with him.
It contains her dreams for him, stories of his birth, and of the
earliest moments of his life. It tells of his friends and enemies,
his hurts and joys, his defeats and accomplishments. It tells of
many of his interactions with parents, family, or friends as he
grew well into his teen years.

As he tells her about the journal, the woman flips lovingly
and excitedly through the pages. At one point she notices that
the handwriting in the journal has changed. He explains to her
that his mother had gifted him with the journal when he went
off to college and at that point, he decided to begin to write in
it as well. The latter half of the journal tells of his thoughts and
experiences as a young man. His first job and first travels, his
friends and enemies, his triumphs and struggles, his plans and
dreams for life, and his deep desire for someone to partner with
him in all of it. He beams as she looks up from the journal with
gratitude in her eyes for the vulnerability of this man she has
just committed herself to. "This is me," he says, "we will

marry, so I want you to have it. I want you to see and know me."

How do you imagine the woman responds? With great joy and honour, of course. She does not toss the journal aside, or leave it closed on a shelf; rather she treasures this journal and reads it regularly, some parts repeatedly. She thinks long about the stories she reads and what they reveal about her fiancé. But never does she begin to think that now she has all she will ever need to know about him contained carefully and precisely in this book. She never stops meeting with her fiancé. Instead she meets with him even more so that they can read the journal together. She laughs and cries together with him at the stories she finds in it, and she continues to open up and share more of her stories with him. She asks him to tell her more about the dreams and plans he has, and she shares with him her dreams and her plans. She wonders at how those can align to fit together in a marriage.

She questions him about the parts of the journal that she does not understand or does not like at first read. She asks him about the parts of his story that are not included in the journal, and he can tell her about those parts now, because they make so much more sense in the context of his full story, and because his trust for her has grown as well.

In moments when he is out of the city on a business trip, or when she is upset about something and not speaking to him, she takes out the journal to remember who he is and why she loves him. When someone who is jealous of her relationship comes to try to tell her other stories about her fiancé, she refers to the journal to confirm or deny what this other person says, and she goes to her fiancé to ask him what he has to say about these things. These interactions over the journal bring the man and the woman into a connection of increasing depth and unity. When the wedding day finally arrives, they are indeed ready and able to become one.

When we can understand the Bible much like the treasured journal in the above story, then we are freed up to embrace it without putting false expectations or false standards upon it. The Bible comes from God and it is an explanation and interpretation of Him and of the unseen realm for us finite creatures, but there is still much mystery left to be unfurled. Written words about or by someone, can never compare with an actual encounter with that person. The Bible provides examples of what interaction with God can look like and how it is made possible, but it does not demonstrate every possible interaction with him, it invites us to interaction. It contains expressions of God's will and his plans within specific times and contexts to help us imagine how he would speak into our specific times and contexts, but the Holy Spirit is needed to help us understand and apply what we find there.

It is important to consider that we desperately need the living voice of God, before we jump in to wrestling with how to interpret the Bible in our own contexts. Before we attempt to decide whether we should understand what we have just read literally, morally, allegorically, or mystically; before we try to detect and label heresy; before we endeavour to decide which word in Uyghur or Wobé would best express the Hebrew word *kaphar* (atonement); before we attempt to disciple that Syrian man who has just received Jesus, along with his two wives, we must know our desperate need for the living voice of God. These tasks mentioned above are all real, all current, and all near impossible to do well if we are not talking with the God-head *as* we read the book he has given us.

In order to read this book with him, we must expect and believe that he still can and still will speak with us. In this book we find that God indeed speaks to his creation—to those who listen as well as to those who do not—and he has been consistently doing so from the very first chapter and continues to speak right into the very last. So, we know God speaks. We find in the story that, though he speaks, only some really listen, and very few respond. It seems the problem is not a God who does not speak; the problem is a humanity that tends to not listen for, or respond to his voice.

In this book, we find God promising that if we seek him with *all* our heart then we *will* find him.[7] We also learn that God is the same today as he was back in the days recorded in the book, and will be the same forever,[8] and so it is safe to conclude that God still speaks openly and regularly to humankind. It is wisdom to conclude that God speaks and *is* speaking—to me, to you, to others. In this story, we learn that those who belong to him know his voice. God reassures us that if we are coming to him and asking for good things, then we will find him (not the enemy) and we will not be given bad things.[9] God tells us that we, like sheep, know our shepherd's voice, and that we will, in fact, run from a stranger's voice.[10] One of my favourite Turkish worship songs contains the line: *My heart was reunited with the owner it had never known.* He is our shepherd who is and always has been speaking, and so, even if we have

[7] Jeremiah 29:13-14
[8] Hebrews 13:8
[9] Luke 11:13
[10] John 10:4-5, 27

never been told of him before, when we finally hear his voice, we *know* him. It feels like a reunion, not an introduction.

The canonization of scripture is also actually proof that God continually speaks, and those who listen are able to discern and respond. The decisions to recognize and confirm the texts that constitute the canon of scripture used today were the result of a long-standing conversation among the people of God, listening together to the voice of God across generations and geographies. Listening together to the voice of God, they were able to recognize and confirm which stories, teachings, letters, and instructions are revelation of and from him and so should be passed on to future generations, and which ancient texts do not carry that imprint. We have this amazing book because of people who listened for and knew the voice of God and so could see him in the texts. They had partaken of his blood and were abiding in him, and so they recognized which written words were inspired by and point to him.

Viewing the Bible as a unique form of revelation, similar to the journal in the above parable, allows us to engage more freely with it, without losing reverence. Armed with solid hermeneutic skills and the knowledge that humankind can hear and know his voice, we are free to translate the Bible into any language, and even multiple versions in any said language. We are free to interpret metaphorical images found in the Bible using other cultural metaphors that, though different, carry similar meaning and relevance to those found in the original stories. For example, a Singaporean missionary to Japan related a story of how a Japanese elderly woman was able to trust Jesus. He explains that "most Japanese, influenced by Buddhism, see the essential reality of life as suffering. Thus 'everlasting life' is equated with 'everlasting suffering'. However, when the gospel was presented...in terms of 'everlasting peace' offered by Christ, she placed her trust in Christ."[11]

We are also free to open the Bible up to textual, cultural, historical, archeological, and internal consistency criticisms, as well as a whole host of other 'isms' because we know the truth of *the* word of God will hold up under any form of criticism. We are free to let anyone read or listen to the Bible—any race, any gender, any age, any status, any mental or emotional capacity, any motivation—any and all are welcome to read, interpret, and try to apply the Bible without fear that the truth of God will cease to be anything other than truth.

Such freedom with the Bible can make us uncomfortable and afraid of what ill-intentioned people could do with these words inspired by the Spirit. The reality is that it is entirely possible to read the Bible and not love it, to read it and not find life, to read it and not find God. Among secularists, atheists, and Islamists, I know people who have carefully read all the pages, and even studied the Bible, but have not become connected to the One who inspired it. But we must not be afraid of the Bible falling into the wrong hands; we must not credit humans with more authority or power than they actually have. The fact that humans can read the Bible and not see the God of love and life does not change the fact that God *is* love and life, or the fact that the Bible testifies to this. Freedom to read scripture, however one sees fit, does not and cannot, negate or alter the truth found in it.

---

[11] Ott, Craig. "The Power of Biblical Metaphors for the Contextualized Communication of the Gospel." Missiology 42.4 (2014): 357-374.

Those who do not find life or love in the Bible either do not hear, or simply do not respond to that first voice that has been speaking to humankind since the garden. Perhaps they read the pages only through the lens of the seen realm and so do not look for, or expect to find an unseen God. Perhaps they read the story but look only for their own ideas of what a god would or should be, according to their accepted standard(s) of what is good or evil. For such, the Bible has no life, no meaning, and really no value. For some, it is not a messenger or a treasured journal that points them to something greater; it is just a book. To read this story as a curiosity, a historical document, a mythology or a fantasy; to read it as a means to prove or disprove a point; to read it to find a confirmation for personally or culturally accepted standards of what is good or bad; to read it for any of these reasons is to completely miss the Bible's reason for being. It is to miss the chance to converse with the One who inspired, authored, and fills it. It is to completely miss God. If, in the pages of the Bible, the source and sustainer of all life, God—as he is, not as he is desired, imagined, or perceived to be—is not sought, then he will not be found.

Sadly, those who are not seeking God at all are not the only ones who can miss him even as they read the pages of the Bible. As we look across the globe at the people of God right now, we see a myriad of differing interpretations and diverse expressions of what we find in this beautiful catalogue of stories, poetry, wisdom literature, and teachings. This is unavoidable, since not one of us has a supra-contextual point of view from which to look at scripture; we necessarily read and interpret and apply through our own cultural and contextual lenses. This could (and should be) a source of richness and a way to mutually build one another up as we together seek to know and understand God in and through our applications and expressions of what we read in the Bible. Yet, so often what we see happening throughout the larger body of Christ, is that people tend to see God only in their own interpretations and expressions of the Bible but then completely miss him in those of others.

I remember how shocked I was when a respected Christian author, speaker, and leader, together with a number of other anointed Christian leaders organized a large conference with the distinct purpose of outright condemning the entire charismatic movement. In their zeal to correct confusing or overextended interpretations and applications of scripture, they had completely missed where God might actually be present and at work within this movement which has dramatically and extensively impacted denominations and traditions throughout the Christian world. I also remember how taken aback I was one day by a couple of brothers who had just recently come to serve together with us in the southeast of Turkey. After a particularly powerful time of prayer together one evening, they pulled me aside to excitedly tell me that they believed I was ready to receive the Holy Spirit. They assumed that because of my denominational background I somehow had no relationship with one of the members of the Godhead.

Of course, it is possible to misunderstand and misinterpret what is there in scripture. Our fleshly nature inclines us to see what we want to see, while making us blind to what we need to see. As I have grown in my Christian faith I recognize that this has certainly happened for me. I daresay that most mature Christians would admit that this has happened for them as well.

It is not possible to entirely control how people read, interpret, and respond to the Bible. We can encourage, exhort, challenge, and question, but at some point we must choose to trust the Spirit to guide us, and others, in the way we should go, and in his timing. Like Paul we must choose to say:

> I press on toward the goal to win the prize for which God has called me heavenward in Christ Jesus. All of us, then, who are mature should take such a view of things. And if on some point you think differently, that too God will make clear to you. Only let us live up to what we have already attained.[12]

Paul encourages us to live according to what we have thus far learned and understood of God, and also exhorts us to not have our minds set on earthly things but on heavenly things. When our minds are set on things above, we are better prepared to discern where God is or is not present in the diverse interpretations and expressions of scripture found across the body of Christ.

Instead of being a place of strength and abundance, the diversity in interpretation and expression in the body of Christ is instead often a place of weakness and a source of great division. The church becomes divided and sick when we cannot see God present and active in others outside of our specific context or our particular theological bent. When we do this, we limit God. We miss how many times in the Bible when we see

[12] Philippians 3:14-16 NIV

that God was for, and with people even when their understanding of him was not fully accurate or not yet complete. The most central example is the nation of Israel. It does not mean we unequivocally accept and embrace all ideas as truth, it just means we choose not to deny that God can be, and indeed is active in contexts and people that we do not expect or do not understand. The people of God, the body of Christ, the temple of the Holy Spirit is so much bigger than whatever small corner of it that we currently find ourselves in. There is mystery, wonder, and beauty to behold if only we can step out of our comfort zones and be willing to trust the sovereignty and guidance of God as we look at and listen to others.

In the next chapter, with the help of a metaphor, we will explore how we can think about and approach one another in ways that propel us towards unity and wholeness without compromising God's standard.

8

And We Pray That All Unity May
One Day Be Restored

*So often Christians believe they have to arrive at complete
doctrinal unity before they can work together. This is unlikely
to occur. Doctrine, of course, is incredibly important but I
have never met two Christians who believe exactly the same
about every issue in the Bible.*
—Brother Yun[1]

*Unity despite diversity is exactly what defines
Christianity as distinct from and antithetical to all
other religious belief systems.*
—R. Alan Woods[2]

*How baffling you are, oh Church, and yet how I love you!
How you have made me suffer, and yet how much I owe you!
I should like to see you destroyed, and yet*

[1] Yun, Hattaway P. *Living Water*. Grand Rapids, Michigan: Zondervan; 2008.
[2] Woods R. *Apologia: A Collection Of Christian Essays*. Wilmington, OH: Rhema
Rising Press; 2007.

I need your presence.
You have given me so much scandal and yet you
have made me understand sanctity.
I have seen nothing in the world more devoted to obscurity,
more compromised, more false, and I have touched nothing
more pure, more generous, more beautiful. How often I have
wanted to shut the doors of my soul in your face, and how of-
ten I have prayed to die in the safety of your arms.
No, I cannot free myself from you, because I am you, alt-
hough not completely.
And where should I go?
—Carlo Carretto[3]

Before I began writing this chapter I had a dream. As usually happens with dreams, most of it faded as the sleep left my eyes but one part was clear and stayed with me. In my dream there were a couple of investigators who were trying to find a particular man and were at the home of a stone carver who claimed he personally knew the man in question, and where to find him. The investigators were suspicious of his claim and wanted to know how he could possibly be so sure. The man got a solemn look on his face and then invited them to follow him into another room. He brought them to his salon, a large room that had been uniquely built with one entire supporting wall being a jagged rock surface. The rock wall was more than a storey tall with some green plants growing out of it as well as a few art pieces placed on it. Across the rock wall surface, many images had been carefully carved. In some places a whole human body could be seen, while in other

[3] Carretto, Carlo. *The God Who Comes*. Darton, Longman & Todd, 1974.

places only parts, and mostly one face was seen repeatedly carved across the whole surface, from different angles and with different emotional expressions. Some of the carvings were very abstract and barely decipherable; others were meticulously detailed and pristine.

As the investigators took in this complex, peculiar, but compelling rock wall, the carver told them that he was certain of the identity of the man they were looking for because he *knew* this man so well. In my dream it wasn't clear what the carver's relationship was to the man in question but it was understood that they were family, maybe his father, or brother, or uncle. The wall carvings were evidence and expression of that deep knowledge. This was a man he knew intimately, a man that he clearly honoured and treasured. Regularly he would carve something of his meditations about this man into the rock wall. Though none of the carvings were complete, some not even particularly good, they were a vast and growing collection.

Looking across the wall at all the carvings, the investigators could potentially piece together a composite of the man in question, but in my dream, that was not the point of the wall. The carver did not bring them to the wall so that they could use the carvings to confirm the identity of the man in question. Rather, he showed them the wall so that they could understand the depth of his knowledge of and love for the man. The carver's deep relationship with the man was confirmation of his claim that he knew him. The wall was simply a tangible, visible reflection of that deep connection. It was evidence that when he said he knew the man, he meant it.

As I thought about this dream and asked God about it, I felt it was a metaphor. In the dream the man in question represents the Godhead, the carver represents the Spirit, and the carvings represent the visible church over the centuries and across the globe. The Spirit knows the divine community intimately and completely because he is a part of it. In Paul's letter to the Corinthians he speaks about the Spirit in a similar fashion, "...the Spirit searches everything, even the depths of God. Who knows a person's thoughts except the spirit of that person, which is in him? So also no one comprehends the thoughts of God except the Spirit of God."[4] It is the Spirit who reveals the Godhead to every church community. The carvings represent what various church communities have received and thus far understood about God and about what he has prepared for humankind, and then given tangible expression to this. "We impart this," Paul continues, referring to what no eye has seen, no ear has heard, and no heart has imagined, "in words not taught by human wisdom but taught by the Spirit."[5]

Some of these carvings by the Spirit are quite abstract, capturing only a strong, rather obvious emotion, or a more pronounced feature, such as a hand or an eye, while other carvings are more concrete and thorough—carefully depicting easily identifiable, polished features and more subtle emotions, such as a look of peace or one of resolution. The metaphorical rock wall with all the Spirit initiated and inspired carvings from the church across time and across cultures is a true masterpiece to behold, and yet there are still carvings to be added to the mix.

[4] 1 Corinthians 2:10-11
[5] 1 Corinthians 2:13

These rock wall carvings are not perfect or complete representations of God, but they offer expressions of deep understanding of, and connection to him, and no other. Those expressions are initiated, and given shape by the Spirit. Each individual carving makes more sense in the context of the rest of the carvings, and only with respect to the carver.

Embracing the blood of Christ is the essential piece for any community to be able to enter into covenantal relationship with the metaphorical carver (the Spirit) and receive revelation of the Godhead. Then as the carver reveals the Godhead to the growing church each carving tends to be nuanced slightly differently from the next since each church community tends to be attracted to, and centre their focus on a particular quality, activity, or promise of the Godhead. Emphasis on the holiness and mystery of God may take the form of an abstract rendering on the rock wall, perhaps just the back of a head or the corner of an imperial looking robe. A revelation of the intimacy and nearness of God may come out as a detailed, close-up carving of expressive, love-filled eyes, or perhaps arms outstretched, as if ready to embrace. An encounter with the power and force of God may elicit a carving of a muscular arm coming out from the rock, or a foot ready to trample on a snake. A persecuted church community might deeply resonate with the suffering God, and so their carving may take the form of a broken, barely recognizable battered face, or perhaps a figure slumped over. A church community that has seen and experienced tremendous provision—physical, emotional, financial, or otherwise—may form a carving of a dazzling, majestic face, with rock polished to perfection. Any of these different carvings can, and likely will evoke a very adverse reaction from any group whose carving looks dramatically, or even subtly different. This happens when people are first focused on what is unclear or missing, what is over or under emphasized, or what initially appears to be distorted or warped in any given carving.

There is a long history of these carvings as humanity has, over time, encountered the one true triune God and has given expression to those experiences and understandings. We now have a very wide breadth of carvings to observe on the rock wall as the Bible—the testimony of God and his provision for humankind—has reached so many more of the cultures of the world and has found unique expression in each. Such incredible richness, the diversity of the church body across time and across space not only gives us a beautiful masterpiece to behold, it also helps us to have a much bigger and far more accurate picture of who God is, and what he has been revealing to humankind about us and about the unseen realm.

Unfortunately, in the church our tendency is not to look at the whole rock wall, but rather to focus primarily, even solely, upon our own particular carving. We tend to be very proud of what our particular carving emphasizes, of its beauty or its accuracy, but then only look briefly and very superficially at other carvings, if we look at all. It is sadly not uncommon for us as Christians, to comment and complain about a carving we have never even looked at for ourselves but have only heard other people's descriptions or opinions of. From these brief, superficial, or second hand glances, we compare other carvings with our own, and then are quick to point out differences, which usually means pointing out what we perceive as *wrong* with the other carving, not what might be *right* with it. In the act of comparison, it is easy to become suspicious, offended, or proud.

When it comes to considering other denominations, other traditions, and other church communities, we often begin with an attitude of criticism. I imagine this is because criticism initially feels easiest and safest. To point out what is missing, unclear, or faulty in something seems to come quite naturally to us. Generally, it is what bothers us that is more readily apparent than what has been done well. It is like coming home and noticing that there is one dirty pan left in the sink but not seeing that the whole house has been cleaned. What is wrong is often more obvious than what is right. Any social media platform provides us with prime examples of how easy and enticing it is to be a critic. Just try walking down a street avoiding all temptation to mentally criticize or make judgments about people based on their appearance or behaviour and we see how easily we become critics. Certainly criticism on some level is necessary; we must be aware of, and fully accept what is wrong if we are ever going to be able to fix it. But when it comes to the things of God, when it comes to the church, criticism as a *first* approach is not usually particularly helpful.

There are a number of reasons for why this is the case. To begin with, criticism assumes, indeed requires, a level of expertise and authority. Yet, if we are truly honest with ourselves, very few of us can claim real expertise or authority, especially when it comes to the things of God. Next, criticism is a form of judgment, in that it places the critic *above* whoever or whatever is being criticized. As Christians we should recognize what a dangerous position this is to be in; Jesus tells us that we will be judged in the same way that we judge, that the measure we use for others will be measured to us.[6] Finally, criticism is often focused predominantly, if not exclusively, on fault-finding, especially in the church context. But if we consider the textbook definition of professional criticism, it includes not only the analysis and judgment of faults, but also the recognition and appreciation of merit. From experience, we observe that fault-finding criticism, while it certainly has a place, rarely seems to yield the fruit it so emphatically promises, that being correction of perceived faults.

When we approach another group beginning with criticism, we are generally on a hunt for that which is wrong or dangerous, and so a desire to listen, understand, show mercy, or find solutions can be set aside, or even outright rejected. As such, using criticism as the starting point, or as a central or preferred way to interact with the 'carving' of another denomination or church community tends to do little more than belittle and discourage, and even has the potential to further reinforce walls of protection which serve to divide. Using criticism as a first approach also has the potential to reinforce pride in the criticizer and likewise reinforce or strengthen walls built to defend, which also serve to divide.

Seeing only what is lacking, what is exaggerated, or what is inaccurate in the carvings of other communities, whether those from different denominational streams or those from different cultural backgrounds, results in division. When we come to believe that our carving is the best carving, perhaps even a perfect rendering and really the *only* carving, then of course we will criticize, resist, and separate from any that do not look exactly like ours. Walls of division get built around and between

[6] Matthew 7:2

diverse interpretations and expressions of the same story, of the same divine mystery. These walls aren't new; they have been forming since the church first originated and have sadly only increased in number and complexity. Thankfully there is (and always has been) some limited exchange between these walls as some walls are low or have open gates. Though many of the walls are high and some have steel reinforcement and barbed wire, while others even have weapons on them. We sadly see a great deal of accusations flying between and across these walls.

The accusations tend to start out fairly simple. One group might accuse another of 'emotionalism', while another group may then accuse them of 'legalism'. The group accused of emotionalism may have a tremendous revelation of the intimacy and closeness of God, of the One who rejoices and sings loudly over his people with gladness, and who quiets them by his love.[7] On the other hand, the group accused of legalism may have a deep fear of God with a profound understanding of holiness, without which, scripture tells us, no one will see God.[8] Certainly neither of these emphases is wrong, but both are incomplete. These accusations, if not kept in check, can become much more severe. One group may accuse another of being 'baseless', claiming that they have no grounding whatsoever in scripture. The accused group may then accuse the other of being 'loveless', believing that a criticism or attack on a particular focus or belief equals hatred, and so, such a group must be devoid of the Spirit.

[7] Zephaniah 3:17
[8] Hebrews 12:14

There are, of course, groups who are clearly outside of scripture, groups who do not know or have completely lost all connection with the Carver, and so do not know or recognize the Godhead—Jesus in particular. For example, Muslims, Buddhists, Jehovah Witnesses, and Mormons all deny the Trinitarian nature of God, a core revelation of who God is, the divine community of love. This denial of the Godhead reveals a lack of connection with the Carver. With such groups, we can pray for, testify to, and trust the power of God's grace to bring clarity and revelation to them. These groups are very different from groups who, while agreeing on the core nature and revelation of the Godhead, differ in terms of interpretation or application of scriptural instructions for living an abundant life while still in this fallen world. What I am addressing here is our tendency to miss that other groups are often *not* completely outside of scripture, and are not actually disconnected from the Spirit. They simply have not seen, understood, or embraced a piece of scripture as we have, or perhaps have a different application or interpretation. That application or interpretation may be causing problems in the community; it may be hindering the abundant life that Jesus spoke of, but it might not mean that they have lost sight of the carver. It could even be that what they have understood is actually more accurate, while *our* particular interpretation or application has been causing problems which we are either blind to, or have chosen to ignore. Jesus taught that we can recognize a tree by its fruit, and so we can assess the validity of an interpretation or application based on the fruit produced. Does it draw people closer to the Godhead or does it increase focus on the flesh? Does it result in increased love for God, self, and neighbour or increased division, animosity, and even hatred? Does it result in abundant life or a return to bondage?

I want to emphasize again that it is possible to be wrong about part of scripture but still know the carver, to still know the Spirit. It is first and foremost his job to "convict the world concerning sin and righteousness and judgment;"[9] our primary job is to abide in him. We must be very careful when we begin to judge another as being completely out of relationship with the Godhead. Are we certain before God of our judgment? Has God instructed us to call out judgment on them; has he actually asked us to even address the issue at all? If we are certain about bad fruit resulting from an interpretation or application of scripture, it is also possible to come to the table with those concerns without any love in our hearts. The consequences of such an approach can be as ruinous as bad fruit from a wrong interpretation, and yet, lacking a fruit of the Spirit does not mean that an entire community or movement is devoid of the Spirit and therefore completely out of relationship with the Godhead. Judging another is dangerous territory and we must tread carefully and wisely.

The walls of division, and the back and forth accusations passing between them are destroying the body of Christ. Paul reminds us that, "the whole law is fulfilled in one word: 'You shall love your neighbour as yourself,'"[10] and then he warns us that if we bite and devour one another, we had better watch out or we will be consumed by one another.[11] He exhorts us to

[9] John 16:8
[10] Galatians 5:14
[11] Galatians 5:15

welcome the one weak in faith, but not to quarrel over opinions.[12] Jude in his letter to believers points out the dangers of those who have snuck in to the church to pervert the grace of God,[13] who follow ungodly, fleshy passions.[14] He explains that it is these who cause division, these who are devoid of the Spirit.[15] But, interestingly, he says to the believers that their response to such troublemakers should instead be to build *themselves* up in faith, keep *themselves* in the love of God, pray in the Spirit, wait for the mercy of Christ, and have that same mercy on those who doubt.[16] He does not invite them to build a wall of defence, or to criticize or accuse. Instead, he invites them to look inward and upward, to expect and then give mercy.

These walls, and the back and forth accusations are also destroying our Christian witness in the world. We must wake up to this. The rest of humankind sees these walls and hears the accusations, and they are repulsed or they mock. God also sees these walls and hears the accusations, and he weeps and he beckons.

These accusations often do not come with evil intent, I believe many are motivated by a sincere desire to protect the body of Christ and defend truth about God. We suppose that by pointing out all that is incomplete, misunderstood, or misrepresented by another group of people who claim to have the person of Christ, we are protecting our flock by defending truth and proving its worth. We genuinely believe that we are doing

[12] Romans 14:1
[13] Jude 4
[14] Jude 18
[15] Jude 19
[16] Jude 20-23

something truly great for God. We tell ourselves that if we don't do it, who will? What we do not realize is that perhaps God's truth does not actually need defending in the way we think it does. Divine, ultimate truth is truth, period. No matter how much or what type of falsehood is tossed around out there, none of it can actually alter truth. Jesus says, "I was born and have come into the world, to testify to the truth. Everyone who belongs to the truth listens to My voice."[17] If we (or others) belong to the truth, then we *will* recognize his voice; and, if we recognize his voice, we *will* know and have the truth. It is actually lies which demand proof and require defence. Only the counterfeit needs, and tries very hard, to prove itself because it will never hold up once put alongside the genuine.

Counterfeit is the business of the enemy of humankind. The central problem of sin is that it is a counterfeit to God's perfect standard and perfect provision. It looks good, and it promises good things, and it may even deliver these things for a time. But the worthlessness and consequences of sin are immediately recognized when confronted with the original, with that which is genuine. Even the most successful criminal would never choose counterfeit dollars if real ones are presented to him; that would be ludicrous! The only reason a criminal uses or manufactures counterfeit dollars in the first place is because he does not have access to genuine currency.

Generally, accusation does not bring about any real change because it is almost exclusively focused on counterfeit. Accusation, in fact, feeds on it, always looking for more places, and more ways to accuse. Counterfeit is not recognized as counterfeit by studying *it;* you can only know what is counterfeit by

<hr>
[17] John 18:33

careful, thorough, and consistent study of the genuine. A skilled jeweller does not bother going about looking for fake jewels—that is a waste of his time. His effort is best put into knowing his craft, working with real jewels. He only needs to deal with fake jewels when he is asked, or if they come across his path. If the majority of our time is spent focused on and seeking out the counterfeit, it is likely that we will begin to no longer be certain about what is genuine. Focus on the counterfeit stirs up confusion, doubt, anger, contempt, and mockery. Focus on the genuine, however, brings about clarity, wonder, respect, confidence, and security. Our primary task as Christians is not to be on the hunt for that which is counterfeit; it is to seek, to know, and to testify to the genuine.

Seeking out what is wrong in order to accuse does not generally bring life and there is good reason for this. Let's consider for a moment where we first see accusation appear in our story. Back in the garden, the first to accuse is the second voice that speaks to humankind. Accusation is his tactic and his nature, and it is also his name—both 'satan' in Hebrew, and 'devil' in Greek mean 'the accuser'. If only we could fully recognize who we are partnering with, and who it is we look like when we accuse others, especially when we accuse others in the body of Christ! God already has one who stands before him day and night accusing the brothers and sisters.[18] He does not need or want that from us.

What God wants and is actively looking for, is intercessors. He is looking for those who, instead of pointing out all the wrong and the pain in the world or the church, are deeply broken by it, and choose to carry it. Those who so desperately

[18] Revelation 12:10

want the wrong and the pain to be gone, that they would actually take it on themselves if necessary, to make it their own, that they may bring it to God in humble supplication so that life can be given in exchange for it. The exchange for whatever is offered up on the altar of sacrifice is always life.

The prophet Ezekiel was one who was deeply broken about the wrong and the suffering he was seeing in the nation of Israel. Israel had come to a shocking level of depravity—extortion, bribery, injustice, abuse of the weak, violence, bloodshed, contempt of family, incest, and child sacrifice. In response to this state, God cries out, "the house of Israel has become dross to me...you have *all* become dross, therefore, I will gather you...as one gathers silver and bronze and iron and lead and tin into a furnace, to blow the fire on it...so I will gather you in my anger...and I will put you in and melt you."[19] The cancerous growth had become monstrous, and cleansing judgment was needed. Yet Israel was not going to be able to withstand the judgment fire that God would pour out to purify the silver, because *all* had become dross, all needed to be burned away. Here, in this circumstance, we learn something of God's heart and his character. We see that God's heart is not for destruction; it is for purification. He wants a nation cleansed and healed, not one destroyed. His heart is for mercy. He is not looking for someone to point out to him all the evil—he already knows that; he is looking for someone to step in to identify with, and repent on behalf of those under judgment, that he may extend mercy. "I sought for a man among them who should build up the wall and stand in the breach before me for the land, that I should not destroy it,"—God was not looking

[19] Ezekiel 22:18-20 italics mine

for an accuser; he was seeking an intercessor. "But," he says, "I found none."[20] Heartbreaking.

Thankfully, there are examples of intercessors in other places in the story. Moses and Paul were two such. Both of these men carried the sin and the pain of the people of God as if it were their own. In astonishing humility, they pleaded on behalf of their brothers and sisters for their salvation, and offered themselves as recipients of God's judgment in place of sinful, rebellious people. When the Israelites had so quickly abandoned the God who had just brought them up out of Egypt, and when they made idols to worship while Moses was up on the mountain, Moses prayed to God: "Alas, this people has sinned a great sin...But now, if you will, forgive their sin—but if not, please blot me out of your book that you have written."[21] Paul prayed a similar prayer for his brothers and sisters, "I have great sorrow and unceasing anguish in my heart. For I could wish that I myself were accursed and cut off from Christ for the sake of my brothers, my kinsmen according to the flesh."[22]

If we look to a more contemporary example, we can find that Mother Teresa was another such intercessor. Like the prophets who wept before God, she, too, understood and lived this kind of sacrificial love.

> Without our suffering, our work would just be social work, very good and helpful, but it would not be the work of Jesus Christ, not part of the redemption—Jesus wanted to help us by sharing our life,

[20] Ibid.
[21] Exodus 32:31-32
[22] Romans 9:2-3

our loneliness, our agony and death. All that He has taken upon Himself, and has carried it in the darkest night. Only by being one with us He has redeemed us. We are allowed to do the same.[23]

Note that she says we are *allowed* to do the same. She considered it a *privilege* to carry the loneliness and pain of others, because she understood that then we become one with them, and one with Jesus. "True love is to surrender," says Mother Teresa, "the more we love, the more we surrender. If we really love souls, we must be ready to take their place."[24]

Oh to know, and to walk in this kind of love and this level of commitment! To be able to sacrificially love brothers and sisters who have ideas about God that make us uncomfortable or upset, to intercede for brothers or sisters who disagree with, accuse, or attack us and our ideas about God, to cry out to God with hope and mercy for brothers and sisters who have lost sight of the Carver. To also be able to sacrificially love enemies, those who are completely outside of the kingdom of light, who do not know, and perhaps do not even want God. Oh to know and be driven by this kind of love, the love that would dare to say *let me be judged; only let them go free.*

Jesus is this kind of love. He is the perfect intercessor.[25] Unlike Moses or Paul, he actually stands in the place of judgment so that we can have life. He is the centre of God's provision for humankind; he is the perfect expression of love. A

---

[23] Teresa, Mother, and Brian Kolodiejchuk. *Mother Teresa, Come Be My Light: the Private Writings of the Saint of Calcutta.* Wheeler Publishing Inc, 2008, p. 220.

[24] Ibid., p. 331.

[25] Hebrews 7:25

shocking challenge comes to us in John's gospel when we read that Jesus commands us to love one another as he has loved us. Shocking, because in the very next line we learn what Jesus means when he tells us to love one another as he has loved us; he means *by laying down our lives.*[26] How many times have we glossed over these words of Jesus, grateful for the sacrifice that he made for us, while completely missing his command for us to do the same. Jesus intercedes, he takes pain and wrath upon himself so that others can go free, and in doing so, he sets a standard for us to live by. We, who are made in the image of God, actually have the capacity to love like this; we can give this kind of love because we experience it; we can love because God first loved us.

Paul understood this standard. "We always carry around in our body the death of Jesus...we who live are always being given over to death for Jesus' sake, so that the life of Jesus also may be manifested...So death is at work in us, but life is at work in you."[27] The writer of the letter to the Hebrews also understood this standard, grasping both its beauty and its weight. In his letter he invites us to consider Jesus who endured the cross for the joy set before him (his bride), and to consider him who endured such hostility from sinners that we might not grow weary in our struggle against sin. Then he points out that we have not yet resisted to the point of shedding our own blood, meaning, we have not yet wrestled with sin in the way or to the extent that Jesus has. This call from the writer of Hebrews is not only a call to accept discipline from God (as we find in the

[26] John 15:12-13
[27] 2 Corinthians 4:10-12

following verses), it is also a call to be willing to suffer sacrificially to see sin dealt with.

Understanding that we are called to sacrificial love as the people of God and the body of Christ, should be a serious heart check for us, a way for us to gauge our motivations and priorities. The spirit of accusation wants the other to be exposed and to be blamed, and it looks for a place for the suffering of sin to land upon. The spirit of love, however, wants the other to be seen and set free, and sacrificial love offers a place for the inevitable suffering of sin to land. Putting on the lens of sacrificial love will dramatically change how we approach one another—other churches, other denominations, other traditions, other cultures, other people—period. This lens will allow us, when we first approach others, to stop asking the question: do they believe and do all the right things? Because in humility we will recognize that, right now, *no one* believes *all* the right things—least of all you, least of all me.

"Now we see things imperfectly, like puzzling reflections in a mirror...all that I know now is partial and incomplete"[28] says the great teacher Paul, but with the expectation that he will one day come face-to-face with God. Then he will see everything with perfect clarity, and will know everything completely. Only in the person of Jesus do we find perfect truth and perfect behaviour; everything else we witness or ascribe to, no matter how deep or how sound, is still only partial, is still shockingly limited. Our hard sought, carefully and communally crafted Christian doctrines, as beautiful, foundational, sound, and necessary as these are, are still only partial and lim-

---

[28] 1 Corinthians 13:12

ited, essential but incomplete. Our myriad of Christian doctrines are the renderings of people looking through a glass darkly.

Recognizing our limitations and imperfections, and the need for intercession rather than accusation, what then is the standard by which we are to understand who is in communion with the Godhead and who is not? A verse I often hear used preceding judgments pronounced against another denomination or group of believers concerning their beliefs and practices is from a letter by the disciple John. He warns the recipients of the letter (and us) not to believe every spirit, for many false prophets have gone out into the world.[29] True. There are entire religions based upon false teachings, often false teachings specifically about Jesus. As such, John invites us to test the spirits (the spirits, not the people), and he then gives us the standard by which we may know if someone belongs to God or not: "By this you know the Spirit of God: every spirit that confesses that Jesus Christ has come in the flesh is from God, and every spirit that does not confess Jesus is not from God."[30] Elsewhere Paul gives us almost the exact same standard: "No one speaking in the Spirit of God ever says 'Jesus is accursed!' and no one can say 'Jesus is Lord' except in the Holy Spirit."[31] This is the standard by which we test the spirits of falsehood.

Dutch pastor Jan Sjoerd Pasterkamp summed it up well when he stated, "Truth is not a teaching. Truth is a person, and if you have that person, you have the truth. And in that person there is always unity."[32] The question we need to be asking

[29] 1 John 4:1
[30] 1 John 4:2-3
[31] 1 Corinthians 12:3
[32] Wilson, Darren, director. *Furious Love*. WP Films, 2010.

when we first approach others is not: do they believe and do all the right things, but rather do they know the Spirit, have they declared Jesus as Lord? If we have Jesus, then we can have unity with one another as Christians. It is a matter of thinking covenantally. When people choose family they make covenantal vows such as *for better, or for worse,* and *in sickness, and in health*; a choice is made to be committed to another no matter what may come, a choice which anticipates disagreement and difficulty. We can approach our brothers and sisters in Christ in a similar fashion, recognizing that as those covenanted to the Lord we have thus been brought into covenant with his whole body.

In Paul's first letter to the Corinthians, he informs them that they bring judgment on themselves if they do not discern the body when they approach the communion table.[33] He is of course referring to the body of Christ, but recognizing his body at the communion table means not only Christ's physical body that was given for us on the cross, but also his spiritual body, meaning the church. At the communion table we recognize our covenantal relationship with Christ, a covenant which inherently includes *everyone* who is also found abiding in Christ. Can we begin to see other communities of Christians as those we are covenanted to—for better, or for worse, in sickness, and in health? Can we choose to together seek to understand all that is necessary for the abundant life, free from the yoke of slavery, by wrestling through scripture together with the Spirit and with each other?

By first recognizing that having the person of Jesus as Lord is really the only standard necessary to unite all Christians, and

[33] 1 Corinthians 11:29

then putting on the lens of sacrificial love, we are able to look at our brothers and sisters much more accurately and far more graciously. Armed with this standard and this heart attitude, we can approach another carving and take the time to ask those connected to it to tell us about it, and then actually listen to what they have to say. We can begin to see and understand, maybe even appreciate, the intent and particular emphasis of another carving. It becomes possible for us to even recognize in another carving something that maybe *we* have misunderstood or missed in our own. This gives us the freedom to openly honour another's focus and intent before trying to wrestle with inaccuracy or lack. Such an approach to those with carvings different from our own creates a space where they may then also be open to learning from the intent, focus, and content of our carvings. By coming together in this way, we not only can grow in our understanding of God, but we can grow in love for one another, and we will improve our testimony to the world around us.

Having this standard to gauge with, and putting on this lens of sacrificial love allows us to look more accurately and graciously not only at our brothers and sisters in Christ, but also at *everyone*. In my current context I am surrounded by people who do not see Jesus as the word of God come in the flesh, and who do not, and quite possibly will never confess him as their Lord. A rock carving from them would not accurately reflect the Godhead because they do not know or engage with the Carver. Yet approaching them with accusation will not bring desired change, and will not bring life. Beginning a connection by trying to tell someone how irrelevant, inaccurate, or wrong their understanding of God is will only serve to belittle and anger them, and may even strengthen their position. Instead of accusation or criticism, perhaps testimony is the better place to begin. By telling another about our natural daily experience of the Carver, about the story we read and love, about the things we have seen, learned, and received, without an agenda to convert, we might just be able to be a bridge of peace and life. If we come without an agenda to convert but only with a desire to testify to what we have seen and lived, to bring glory to God and to offer life, then, if what we share does not persuade another, we can rest in remembering that truth does not need defending. We can also rest in the fact that it is God himself, it is the Spirit who beckons, convicts, and persuades. We only testify and love sacrificially.

I am also surrounded by many people who joyfully and fully confess Jesus as their Lord. We have all met and committed ourselves to the same person, Jesus, and we all know the Carver, the Spirit. Many of these people have experiences, understandings, and expressions of God that are identical, or at least very similar to mine, but others have ones that are dramatically, sometimes even offensively different from mine. Their different carvings are, of course, biased, incomplete, and slightly inaccurate in places, but then, so is mine. By talking to one another, we gain so much. As we each are confronted with new perspectives, new questions, and new challenges, we are forcibly driven to look again at the Bible, again at our carvings, and to meet again with the Carver. We are forced to ask him to help us understand the truth about carvings that look different from ours or ones that make no sense to us. We need the Spirit's help as we look at scripture so that we can together assess where there is error or merit in another's carving or in our own.

The beauty of all of this is that there is not one person mentioned above (whether they know Jesus or not) that I would not sit down and have a conversation or a friendship with, should they also be open. Not one. In his letter to the Romans, Paul invites them, and us, to live peaceably with all people, as far as it depends on us.[34] The part that depends on us is to make sure *our* lenses and *our* motivations are pure. The lenses and motivations of the other person are not our responsibility. Later in the same letter Paul warns us not to pass judgment on the servant of another—that is simply not our job on earth. It is before his own master that a person will stand or fall.[35] God is the master, and he will decide between the sheep and the goats, between the wheat and the tares, because that is his job, not ours. He is the master; he is the judge. Our job is, first and foremost, to be sheep who listen and respond to his voice and to be wheat that yields the fruit of the Spirit—love, joy, peace, patience, kindness, goodness, faithfulness, gentleness, and self-control.[36]

We are one in the Spirit, we are one in the Lord.
We are one in the Spirit, we are one in the Lord.
And we pray that all unity may one day be restored.
And they'll know we are Christians by our love, by our love;
Yes, they'll know we are Christians by our love.

We will work with each other, we will work side by side.

[34] Romans 12:18
[35] Romans 14:4
[36] Galatians 5:22-23

We will work with each other, we will work side by side.
And we'll guard each man's dignity,
and save each man's pride.
And they'll know we are Christians by our love, by our love;
Yes, they'll know we are Christians by our love.
—Fr. Peter Scholtes

9

Brother Let Me Be Your Servant

*God intends to bring to pass a reconciled creation in
which humans reflect in their relationship to each other
and the universe around us the reality of the triune God.
God's actions are aimed at establishing the reconciled
community of love as the human reflection of the social
trinity—the divine nature—which is love.*
—Stanley Grenz[1]

*In an atmosphere of security and trust, persons are likely to
be more ready to change. The child who trusts the mother,
lets go and takes the first unaided step.*
—Harvey and Lois Seifert[2]

*Love is simply the name for the desire
and pursuit of the whole.*
—Plato[3]

[1] As quoted in: Pinnock, Clark H. *Flame of Love a Theology of the Holy Spirit.*
IVP Academic, 1996.
[2] Job R, Shawchuck N. *A Guide To Prayer.* Nashville, Tenn.: Upper Room; 1988.
[3] Plato. *Symposium.* [S.l.]: Weyland Easterbrook; 2020.

In the last of the above quotes, Plato was referring to romantic love and the pursuit of a person's other half and he was actually onto something; it was just that his vision was a little too small. This story that we find ourselves in begins with a good creation—a beautiful unified system, where each part interacts with, supports, sustains, and receives from the other, and where each part is a visible and tangible reflection of some aspect of the Godhead. The story continues by telling us about the horrific division of that unified whole, and then about God's provision for unity to be possible again. The story ends with a promise that the creation will be cleansed and freed of everything that refuses God's provision (and thus refuses God), until all that remains is a perfectly restored whole. God's heart and his plans are for this restored whole, a place of complete belonging and perfect unity, a place where all will finally be one in desire and purpose. This is a place of mutual submission and empowerment. The restored whole will be a place of perfect love. So, love is indeed the desire and pursuit of the whole, and also the realization of it.

We have looked in depth at how our story begins and ends with unity. In the process we have seen how broken and divided we have all become and how impossible our circumstances really are. From there we have considered different aspects of God's provision for humankind to make it through to the end of this current story and to again experience unity. His first provision was creating humankind in his image, which means we were created in and for community. He then provided his standard to keep us all together as one, and in that he gave us blood as provision for life and for connection. He then gave us the Son and he also gave us the Spirit, and he gifted us with texts that record and testify to all of this. We looked at how different understandings and applications of these texts have led to great disunity but that God has made provision for that as well, having given us the Spirit of truth. In this chapter we will look more closely at one more aspect of God's provision for humankind in order for unity to be possible.

One of God's perhaps most amazing gifts of provision for us to make it to the final chapter of this current story is the gift of each other, and the divine gift of healing so that we can actually connect with one another in wholesome ways. God has designed the human body with the capacity to repair and restore that which has been damaged or broken, given the right conditions. No matter how knowledgeable or skilled they may be, doctors do not heal a body. What they do is provide the right conditions for that healing to happen, for it is the body which heals itself. God has designed the human psyche with the same healing capacity if given the right conditions. Just as the physical body heals itself with help, so, too, can the soul heal itself with the right help. If we receive God's provisions, then we have accepted and have made room for the conditions necessary for healing to happen, and for the restoration and new life of the body, soul, and spirit.

We were created as entirely relational creatures, each of us a living, moving representation of a trio (father, mother, and child), and as such, so much of who we are is formed only in and through relationship. We actually do not come into the world as fully formed selves. Our brains do not even finish developing until we are into our twenties since so much of the brain's development happens only as it engages with the world around us. Our most crucial development as humans cannot and does not happen without connection to other people. Our identity is "constituted in, through, and by [our] interactions with others...Who [we are] is revealed in, through, and by [our] interrelationships with others."[4] Since our soul, or our personality, is developed in relationship, it should not surprise us that damage to our soul also comes via relationship. The more intimate the relationship (i.e. father, mother, spouse, sibling, etc.), the greater the potential damage. Considering that damage to our souls comes through relationship, it is not surprising then that healing of our souls also comes through relationship as well. Connection to God, and then healthy, intimate, diverse community are the main conditions necessary for repair and restoration of a soul. The fruits produced by the Spirit in believers—love, joy, peace, patience, kindness, goodness, faithfulness, gentleness, self-control—form the pillars of any healthy community, and forgiveness and reconciliation circle us back to these pillars when we lose our way. Each of these is a transformative gift given to humankind to allow us to live in unity.

As mentioned in chapter two, the breeding ground of the widespread evil that we often, if not always, see in the world today, begins with rejection, neglect, or abuse that happens, usually in our closest relationships, and most notably in infancy or childhood. Damage that comes to us when we are small has a particularly devastating effect because it comes at a time when we are still discovering who we are and learning how we are supposed to relate with other humans. It is the time when our view of ourselves and the world around us is being

---

[4] Olthuis, James H. The Beautiful Risk: *A New Psychology of Loving and Being Loved.* Wipf & Stock, 2006.

formed. Rejection as a child by a primary caregiver, for example, can result in 'rejected' becoming our identity, 'self-protection' or 'isolation' becoming our default for relating with others, and 'dangerous' or 'foreign' becoming the way we view the world. Or, neglect as a child can result in 'worthless' becoming our identity, 'neediness' or 'aggression' becoming our default for relating with others, and 'uninterested' or 'inaccessible' becoming the way we view the world. We may recognize patterns or habits currently present in our lives which are damaging, but if our default settings are off, we may not be aware that these are likely connected to, or even a direct result of a false understanding of our identity or about how we relate to the people around us.

Damage done to us in close relationships can impact not only our view of ourselves or others but also our view of God. He created fatherhood, motherhood, marriage, sibling relationships, and friendships all in order to help us have a tangible, visible understanding of what he is like and how we can relate to him. But when our experience with earthly fathers, mothers, spouses, siblings or friends is unhealthy or harmful, our view of God can be (and frequently is) distorted. Damage done to us in our most intimate relationships impacts our core, the very essence of who we are as humans and harms our foundational understanding of all relationships. Healing that comes through relationship can then, in the same way, impact our very core, and repair any broken understanding of God, ourselves, and the world. As Christians, we simply cannot afford to ignore or overlook the tremendous impact that foundational relationships have upon us, both positive and negative. Focus on relationship should be *central* in all our approaches to church or ministry.

As we seek to identify and wrestle with that which causes division in the world, the place to begin is the healing and restoration of brokenness in individuals through God-given healthy community. This is not only to mend current circumstances but also to protect future generations by preventing cycles of pain and hurt from continuing. As we seek to bring healing to others, when we choose to listen and accept people as they are and create a space that is accepting of hurt and shame, inevitably we will begin to see how common and widespread brokenness really is, and we will hopefully begin to recognize and acknowledge the brokenness in us, too.

When we begin to share our stories we will inevitably find points of connection, and start to see just how much we actually have in common with those from different cultures, socioeconomic status, or theological camps. Once we find these points of connection, we can, and will, enter more into the lives of others, and they in turn will enter more into ours. We will begin to feel that we really do belong to one another. When seeds of brokenness are discovered, they can be uprooted from our hearts so that they can then be replaced with truth; truth which tells us that we are seen, accepted, cleansed, and made new, truth that is not only spoken but also experienced. When we experience this kind of transformation, we would want others to experience the same. We begin to understand that we possess the ability to give life and hope in this world by helping others to be seen, accepted, cleansed, and made new, regardless of what they have done or where they come from. We can and will want to create and foster more communities which are safe enough for such roots of brokenness to be exposed, and healthy enough that such roots can be dealt with and replaced with seeds of truth and life. I believe that learning how to create such communities is *everything*.

When we join with God in his provision for unity, then we become increasingly aware of and more deeply concerned about the nature and quality of relationships within and among our church communities or ministries. We also become more aware of and concerned about relationships within and among cultures and nations. Understanding that we are part of the same creation, part of the same greater whole, helps us realize that what we do impacts far more than just ourselves. Our actions and reactions, whether for good or bad, powerfully affect other people and communities, the environment and the creatures in it, and, of course, God. When we recognize that we are inextricably bound to one another, bound to *all* others, we can begin to understand that the shame or pain of one is actually the pain or shame of all, and that the freedom or success of one actually belongs to all. The only reason I can be unaffected by the suffering of another human is if I don't see them as part of me.

The writer of the letter to the Hebrews tells us that not one of the heroes of the faith mentioned in his letter received the promises for which they suffered or even died because, "God had provided something better...that apart from us they should not be made perfect."[5] When God looks on us, he sees not only individuals and their stories, he sees humanity as a whole and

5 Hebrews 11:40

the overarching story in which all of our sub-stories intersect and connect.

When I read about genocides, wars, slavery, sex trafficking, and the like, I mourn at the utter depravity of humanity, and feel the weight of what we can, and have indeed become in our brokenness, selfishness, and blindness. Similarly, when I read stories of real-life heroes and overcomers, I marvel at the tenacity, beauty, and strength of the human spirit, and I see that God has not yet fully withdrawn his hand from us. How we react to adversity in our own lives and respond to others in their pain and shame says a great deal about where our focus and our heart is. We may ignore pain or shame, pretending that we do not know, see, or feel it. We may condemn and judge it, calling for more suffering and pain in the name of justice or perhaps in a spirit of revenge. Or we may embrace it, no matter how ugly or terrifying it may be, and seek to enter in and carry it, crying out that it should not be this way. We can bring it all to God to learn what it is that has brought us to such a place, and then we can trust and expect that he will show his provision given to redeem such circumstances.

Building healthy communities is the way to carry and redeem the pain in this world but, sadly, healthy communities are few and far between. Unfortunately, this is just as true when it comes to the church. I believe this is because a healthy community requires more than superficial connection. Meeting somewhat regularly to talk about a passage of scripture, to sing songs or have a barbecue does not reflect a relationship of depth. Knowing the good, the bad, and the ugly, fighting for and alongside one another, being committed to submitting to one another's strengths, while seeking ways to support and cover one another's weaknesses—that is true community. Such community requires a level of vulnerability, humility, courage, and commitment that is often uncomfortable, risky and costly. And so, it is rarely experienced.

I believe that healthy community is not a place of perfection. It is simply a diverse, rag-tag group of people who have chosen to receive God's provision and are willing to be vulnerable, encouraging, and challenging with one another, and committed to battling the accuser together. This leads me to share my experience of intense community in Turkey, which has been a place of both tremendous struggle and great breakthrough.

When I was first invited to work with a ministry training program based out of the local church in Turkey, I felt excited and privileged to get to be involved in training up local leaders. I presumed that I would be helping with administrative tasks such as organizing program schedules and ministries, or dealing with finances. I also expected I would be doing some teaching on various topics, and that I would have lots of fun hanging out socially with participants. Little did I know what was also awaiting me.

While I was, of course, involved with the above tasks, I found myself involved in many others which I had not anticipated. I also found that administration, teaching, and socializing were not the most pressing tasks, nor were they the ones that had much long term impact in the lives of participants. These tasks were not what took up the bulk of my time or energy. The things I was faced with were conflict resolution; attempting to counsel people through addictions, complicated sin issues, depression, or suicide; praying for and expecting healing (physically, emotionally, mentally, or spiritually); and attempting to be a bridge of clarification and peace between students, teachers, or church leaders with conflicting views.

This ministry training program was born out of a partnership between the local church and foreign ministers and is set up in such a way that repairing damage to the soul is what the leadership team is primarily and consistently engaged with. Of course, there are weekly seminar style classes, which provide foundational knowledge about scripture, collective Christian theology, and a variety of practical ministry topics; such knowledge is a necessary foundation. But for a participant to be a healthy minister, it is simply not enough. There must be ample opportunity to apply, to experience and to obey what is being learned. And so, afternoons in the program are spent in prayer or in various outreach and mercy ministries, and participants regularly travel to other tiny fellowships around the country to visit and encourage more secluded or isolated believers. The final few weeks of the program are spent in cross-cultural outreach in any number of neighbouring nations.

Knowledge is the foundation; application is the necessary next step. But then there is something more still needed: the character to be able to apply knowledge appropriately and to be able to walk in love and honour in ministry and in life. The character component of the training program is perhaps the most important and also the most difficult piece to deal with effectively. In order to give opportunity for character growth, program participants live in community (guys together in one apartment, girls in another, and a couple or a family in another apartment or together with some of the singles, depending on participant numbers) and they all function together as a community every day of the week. They take classes together, serve together, travel and do outreach together, pray and worship together, and socialize together.

The program is open to Turks as well as Turkish speakers, so each year we will have not only Turks but others from a variety of nationalities including Kurdish, Iranian, Armenian, Syriac, Afghan, Kazakh, Kyrgyz, or the occasional European or North American. Participants in this program get to encounter people who are outside of their normal experience, people who look or think differently from them, people who are perhaps even considered enemies according to their ethnic backgrounds. This is volatile territory, and things can, and do, get very messy. But this is also the beauty of it. Things that are hidden and not yet exposed to light remain as they are, untouched and unchanged. But when one comes into a tight community like this one, hidden things simply cannot remain hidden for long. As they are exposed, we can then together learn what to do with them and how to overcome them.

Participants often join the program with a church recommendation, and so, when difficult situations arise involving a particular participant, these tend to come as a surprise to the sending church. In fact, as a program, we have received some criticism because of the number of problems that come up with participants; the misunderstanding being that the program has somehow made people behave badly. But the conditions of the program only bring to the surface what is already present, whether good or bad. Far more than our day-to-day actions, it is our reactions to new or difficult circumstances which reveal our hearts. Living in community makes it much more difficult, if not impossible, to hide things like addiction, anger, depression, doubt, fear, jealousy, pride or any number of other ways we attempt to deal with pain or difficulty. Living in community provides opportunity for things to surface that we may not even know exist in our hearts. If it is a healthy community, then it provides a safe space of grace and the opportunity to find more effective ways to deal with those things which surface.

In most church communities, we can generally keep much of who we really are hidden, the parts of us that we are ashamed of, or maybe are not totally aware of. We do this either by choosing to interact only on Sundays with the community, or by jumping to another community when things get uncomfortable. In our ministry training program this is not possible. In order to graduate one must continue for nearly a full year, through new and challenging circumstances, day in and day out, with the same group of people. Participants get to see many sides of each other, both positive and negative. When conflict inevitably arises, a great deal of importance and time is given to sitting down and talking things out. With clear, mediated communication, core issues can be assessed and new ways of thinking and relating can begin to be taught and modelled as hidden strengths and capacities also have the opportunity to come to the light.

For example, I remember sitting down one evening with a participant as she absolutely raged. Initially she raged about the way the other girls in the program wanted to spend food allowance funds each month, which branched into fury over where laundry was hung or how common living spaces were used, and continued from there. As I listened and asked questions, it became clear that this rage was not really about the kind of food being purchased or the way the salon was being used. Rather, deep wounds of rejection in her were being triggered and reinforced. Armed with this new recognition, this participant began to understand that rejection was an old lie that had been tainting her view of herself and others for a long time, and that God had different truths to speak over her. It was an opportunity for her to learn to identify her needs and emotions, and to communicate those in more effective ways than withdrawal or rage. The other participants also benefited from this new perspective; it was an opportunity for them to have more compassion for this participant and to learn to think of different ways to interact with her that would not reinforce a false lens of rejection.

In another instance, I remember a participant who initially made others uncomfortable with a constant need and pressure for affirmation and approval. There was a deep insecurity and desperation which came across as pride or occasionally contempt. Such behaviour served to push people away from him, which in turn only increased his need to be seen and approved of. The moment a member of the leadership team identified this deep need and began to acknowledge it, finding genuine reasons to approve of his core identity, this participant immediately began to relax; his physical posture even began to change.

Healthy community gives opportunity for reactions (not just actions) to be exposed and then analyzed to discover root needs that are not being met, or being met in unhealthy ways. It then can be a place where appropriate ways to address those needs can be demonstrated and learned. We see stories similar to the above two play out time and time again in our ministry program. Sadly, not every story turns out so well. The mere exposure of an unhealthy behaviour or coping strategy does not guarantee victory over it. Not every person is ready for the next steps, and some do not even want to be free yet because the change can feel too costly. Occasionally, we have to ask a participant to leave the program until they are ready and/or willing to face their own sin, or face forgiving sin done to them. Giving space for what has been hidden in the darkness to be exposed to light is the first necessary step on the road to freedom and abundant life. Healthy community is a grace of God which allows us to know ourselves better. It allows us to see if the cancer of sin has taken root somewhere, while also giving us opportunity to discover hidden strengths, and equipping us with new relational skills and capacities. It also allows us to experience different sides of God as we walk through these things together with him.

It was not only the ministry training program I became a part of that helped to expand and reshape my view of healthy community; it has actually been my whole experience of being in Turkey. Moving to another country was possibly the best thing to ever happen to my relationship with God and my growth as a person. I was born and raised in Canada where, growing up, I was mostly surrounded by people who shared my culture, my economic status, my connection to Jesus, and my particular theological bent. High school and university were the first steps into a world beyond my Christian bubble and, while I did meet amazing people of different faiths and cultures, my deepest and most consistent connections remained with those most similar to me. Moving to Turkey brought me into a world where those connections no longer existed, and I was forced to expand my worldview.

My roommates over the years in Turkey have been from a wide spectrum of nationalities (American, Turk, Swede, Fin, Romanian, South African, Iranian, Korean, Brit, and Arab-Turk). These roommates and my many coworkers over the years, have also come from very diverse church backgrounds (Charismatic, Orthodox, Non-denominational, Pentecostal, Conservative, Reformed, Presbyterian, Southern Baptist, Catholic, or newer believers who do not associate with any particular stream), or from no church background, or even from another faith.

Surrounded by such diversity, something struck me even early on. Though we were so different, and profoundly disagreed about many things, these people became close friends, and even family to me. Though their experience and understanding of God was sometimes dramatically different from mine, living and serving together meant we had to work it out. Confronting me with new challenges, new ways of looking at the world, and new ways of relating with people, God was able to show me places in my heart where I had begun to believe untruths about myself, about others, and about him.

An example of this came early on in my time in Turkey. I remember one roommate who, to me, felt very needy. She regularly sought acknowledgement and validation, and expected a great deal of attention and care when she was sick or feeling down. Initially, I saw this need and desire as weakness and even looked down on her. But through scripture, God began to show me that *he* did not look down on the needy; rather they had a special place in his heart. And in conversations with middle-eastern friends, I began to see how interdependence could be considered a strength. God revealed to me that I had placed independence and self-reliance almost at the level of idolatry, which affected my relationship with my roommate, and with him. I had believed a lie that independence was superior. But through these experiences in Turkey, God was able to show me that dependence is valued, even prized by him.

You do not have to move to another country to come to a deeper understanding or experience of community. A simple willingness to let others into your world who are not exactly like you is enough. To choose to become more vulnerable and more real in the communities that we currently find ourselves in, to be willing to commit more fully to a group of others where we embrace and wrestle with the good, the bad, and the ugly until we overcome, is a tremendous act which will have far reaching impact. I am grateful that God knows us so much better than we know ourselves, so, if we ask him, he will always guide us to the kind of community that will transform us—if we will allow him. He will guide us to those also desperate for this kind of community. If we ask and will allow him, God will always lead us to the greater whole that we may better know who we are and who he is.

10

Bind Us Together Lord

And calling to him a child, he put him in the midst of them and said, "Truly, I say to you, unless you turn and become like children, you will never enter the kingdom of heaven. Whoever humbles himself like this child is the greatest in the kingdom of heaven. Whoever receives one such child in my name receives me."
—Matthew 18:2-5

It must be possible that the soul made
Should absolutely meet the soul that makes;
Then, in that bearing soul, meet every other
There also born, each sister and each brother.
Lord, till I meet thee thus, life is delayed;
I am not I until that morning breaks,
Not I until my consciousness eternal wakes.
—George MacDonald[1]

---

[1] Job R, Shawchuck N. *A Guide To Prayer*. Nashville, Tenn.: Upper Room; 1988.

In our pursuit of the whole, God guides us to encounter increasingly diverse people and places, and theological understandings. This pursuit motivates us to seek to build communities composed of these diverse groups and to also build bridges among them. We have seen that central to this pursuit is believing and receiving God's provision and knowing and responding to the voice of the Spirit as we engage in the Bible and with one another. We have looked at the benefits of avoiding the tendency to criticize when first approaching others and the necessity of choosing the humble path of loving intercession instead of accusation. We have also looked at how healing which comes in and through community is God's provision to us. In this chapter we will consider a final necessary piece in building healthy community.

Regardless of whether a community is culturally, socially, economically, or theologically diverse or not, we should find present each of the sub-groups of the trio that every human being represents, i.e. mothers, fathers, and children (brothers and sisters). If it is a healthy community, each of these sub-groups will not only be present, but will also be recognized, active, and celebrated. For us to be able to overcome challenges that come with trying to live in diverse community, to recognize truths about God, about ourselves, or about one another, and to become better and stronger individuals, we need all of these sub-groups to be given place. This is because each of them has a unique and essential voice; each brings something of tremendous value to the greater whole.

In this story, God's central place for demonstrating the kind of love and community that exists within himself and the initial building block of all humanity, is family. In the Trinity, no person is any less God than the others; no person is any less valuable, any less powerful, any less knowledgeable, any less worthy, any less *anything* than the others. Since humanity was created to reflect the profound unity of the Godhead, we must then recognize that men, women, and children should be acknowledged as having something of value and significance to contribute to the greater whole. Frequently, two of these voices are received far less (if at all) than the other. When one or more of these voices is missing, ignored, or oppressed, it is a sad loss to the greater whole, and such communities will be (and frequently are) weaker for it.

From what we observe throughout the history of humankind, we know that the male voice is given prominence in almost every culture, every society, every denomination, and every community. This Bible likewise overflows with the male voice. There are plenty of examples of how various men have spoken into circumstances or have led families, communities, or nations. Included are very detailed accounts of the results, both good and bad, of how these men spoke or led. As such, I do not believe we need to spend too much time expounding on the importance or necessity of the male voice, since that seems to be a given; but we will focus more on what this voice brings to community.

Generally speaking, the male voice tends to be one that brings vision, purpose, identity, and security. It is a voice that can bring life and focus to our communities, telling us who we are and to whom we belong, where we are heading and what we need to do. But when this voice is disconnected from the Godhead and his standard, it sadly becomes tainted or even perverted, and thus does not bring life to the community. When thus disconnected, the male voice can become aggressive, possessive, or controlling. When this happens, the potential is there for individuals and communities to feel disempowered, oppressed, or even hostile. Such an environment is ripe for division. If disconnected from the Godhead, we also observe that the male voice can become withdrawn or aloof, and sometimes even completely absent. When the male voice is passive, distant, silent, or just plain missing, the potential is there for individuals and communities to be left wrestling for identity and purpose, and floundering in insecurity. We desperately need this voice to be present, and we need it to be untainted by being deeply connected to the Godhead, aware of and accepting of his provisions. The male voice can and should be one that emboldens, equips, mobilizes, and steadies individuals and communities: a voice that brings direction, motivation, and stability.

As we look at the history of humankind, we see that the voice of woman is far less obvious: it is difficult to find and to recognize. This is because it is a voice that has often been, and continues to be, ignored or even actively silenced, in families, in churches, in ministries, and even in entire societies. We find that women, in general, also do not have a prominent place in scripture. Much less is written about or to them, and rarely is a female (with the exception of Esther, Deborah, Ruth, and others) the hero or central figure in a story. How then are we to understand what this voice brings to the community?

We can begin by recognizing that, interestingly, in the Bible, the person of the Holy Spirit is also not particularly obvious. Compared with the Father and the Son, relatively little is written directly, and specifically about the Spirit. He is slightly more difficult to find and to recognize. The Spirit's presence is generally implied or hinted at rather than outright identified. But this does not mean that he is not there, or that he is any less important, authoritative, or necessary than the Father or the Son. He is simply more mysterious, and depicted with metaphors that are a bit more abstract. So too, women are a bit more mysterious, with the female presence in this story tending to be a bit more abstract. You have to look for it, but it is there, and it is significant.

In scripture, the nation of Israel is referred to as female, as is Jerusalem, Babylon, and the church. In Solomon's proverbs, we find that both the tempter's voice and wisdom's voice are female. I do not think that the use of female pronouns in reference to each of these is purely coincidental; it is not just poetic license or simply a point of grammar. This piece has been put into the story to help us recognize that women indeed have a presence, have a voice, and not just in the immediate family but in the greater whole. In order to consider the significance of placing the female voice into the story in such a metaphorical manner, let's consider for a moment the unique physical position in a family that God created the female to be. Physically speaking, a man gives life, and a child receives life; but a woman both receives and gives life. She is a physical bridge between father and child, receiving something, uniting it with something of hers, then containing and nurturing it before finally releasing it into the world. She is the uniting piece in every trio.

I find this to be a profound metaphor to help us look at the overall place of a woman's voice, not just in a family, but in communities and whole societies. A woman receives and responds, but she also communicates and teaches. A woman ponders what has been given to her, analyzes and discerns, summarizes and organizes, and then releases something new and significant into the community. Women have a voice, and it is a powerful one. Woman's voice is so powerful, in fact, that God had to specifically command the Israelites not to take women from the peoples around them for marriage because he knew that these women would draw the people to follow their false gods.[2] Solomon is a prime example of this. He was possibly the wisest man who ever lived, a powerful and stately king, and yet the voices of ungodly women in his life were enough to pull him away from God. In scripture we regularly find places where women miss God's voice and actually cause others to deviate from the right path, such as with Eve inviting Adam to eat with her, or with Sarai[3] suggesting Abram sleep with her servant. Delilah[4] and Jezebel[5] are examples of women who openly refused God's voice and so led others into ugly division and bloodshed. Clearly women have a powerful and effective voice and so need to be careful to use this gift wisely, to bring truth and life, not deception or division.

It is vital that woman is careful to receive from the Godhead, that she may be the right voice in the world. We find examples in the story where women's voices were indeed powerful forces for good. Both Abigail[6] and the unnamed wise woman from Abel of Beth-maaca[7] spoke with such wisdom

[2] Deuteronomy 7:3-4
[3] Genesis 16:2
[4] Judges 16:4-22
[5] 1 Kings 21:5-16
[6] 1 Samuel 25:14-35
[7] 2 Samuel 20:16-22

and honour that they were able to prevent massive bloodshed from happening, commanding circumstances to take a different path. In other places we find women like Esther[8] or Pilate's wife[9] using their voices to reveal much needed truth in critical circumstances, and to give directions concerning what should be done.

We also find in the story that Jesus communicates to women, and trusts and expects them to use their voices to bring life and truth to others (male and female). In the writings of the disciple John, we find Jesus having one of his most theologically deep conversations with a woman. He reveals to her that he is the awaited Messiah, and he speaks to her about the Spirit (before he speaks to his disciples about him). This woman gets up from that conversation to tell her whole town about Jesus, and brings them to him. Jesus does not hinder her as she leaves to go tell others about him, nor does he send a disciple to go and do the task, or even to accompany her in this task. Rather, as she is off to preach the good news, Jesus takes a moment to delight in the harvest that is coming.[10] After his resurrection, Jesus shows himself to Mary Magdalene, and gives her the duty to go and tell the disciples that he is risen.[11] Considering Jesus' example, a question we should ask ourselves as Christians is how is the voice of women being fed, protected, and given place in our communities and ministries?

Some things that have hindered, and continue to hinder this voice from having due recognition in our communities come

[8] Esther 7:3-7
[9] Matthew 27:19
[10] John 4:7-42
[11] John 20:16-18

out of interpretations of the letters of Paul. We can easily over-look the fact that Paul was writing to address specific situations that were causing conflict and division in the body. He was writing to call churches out on issues that were pulling people away from Jesus and/or from one another, and to give them counsel about how to move in a different direction. In his letters to different communities Paul writes some things which, if taken out of the context of a particular letter, appear to conflict with things he has written in other letters. This is certainly true when it comes to women. We use what Paul teaches in his letters for our current contexts but it is important that we understand his overarching aims and goals so that we can avoid getting side-tracked or pulled down into sub-points.

For example, in one letter Paul says women should remain silent in church, but in another he expects that women will be openly prophesying during a church meeting. In one letter he says it was the woman who was deceived first and became a sinner, but then in another he says that sin came into the world through one man, Adam. In one letter he says a woman will be saved through childbearing, and yet in another, he says it would be better for women to remain single. Paul is not contradicting himself; these seeming inconsistencies are because these points that Paul is making are not his main points but are there to serve or expand on other overarching, more central points. Paul is addressing issues such as chaos and disunity in church gatherings, false teachings that come out of cultures which followed gods and goddesses, or an earthly versus a heavenly focus of certain church communities.

The instructions given in Paul's letters are always serving a higher purpose, that of helping people to understand the way of unity, the way of reconciliation with God and with one another. In his letter to the Galatians, Paul says, "There is neither Jew nor Greek, there is neither slave nor free, there is no male and female, for you are all one in Christ Jesus."[12] Paul talks about Christ having torn down the dividing wall of hostility so that we, all of humanity, can be one new person.[13] Paul's words as recorded in the Bible are provision for communities to help them live in unity by addressing circumstances at hand, and always with the fundamental underlying principle of love, meaning the sacrificial, humble, self-giving love that we find in the Godhead.

A few specific parts of Paul's writings have been, and often are used as a basis for dividing men and women, for giving them separate roles, and in some communities, even separate value. Let's look at a passage in his first letter to the Corinthians.[14] If we look carefully at this passage through the lens of provision (for unity), we actually find a basis for profound connection and empowerment for men and women. Paul writes that the source and the glory of woman is man, the source and glory of man is Christ, and the source and glory of Christ is God.[15] Let's set aside the man and woman piece for just a moment, and consider the Father and Son relationship. The Son of course, submits and fully surrenders to the Father, but if we look at the whole of scripture we see that actually, so does the Father to the Son. As the Son submits his will and gives glory

[12] Galatians 3:28
[13] Ephesians 2:15
[14] 1 Corinthians 11
[15] 1 Corinthians 11:3

to his Father, the Father in turn gives glory and surrenders authority, *all* authority, over to the Son.[16] The Son surrenders to and glorifies the Father, and the Father, in giving over all authority, surrenders to and glorifies the Son. It is a give and take relationship, one of mutual love, empowerment, and glorification, not an oppressive hierarchy. Placing the male/female relationship in direct correlation with this Father/Son relationship is remarkable actually. The male/female one is then also not an oppressive hierarchical one, but one of reciprocal surrender, love, empowerment, and glory.

Paul continues his point about unity by noting that men should not disgrace their head (or source), nor should women disgrace theirs. What he is saying is that man was made through and for Jesus,[17] and so, in the purposes and heart of God, man is not independent of or separate from Jesus, because outside of Jesus there is no life. Paul goes on to point out that woman came from man and was made for man; he does this so that we do not miss the fact that man and woman are inextricably bound up with one another. We were never meant to be divided, we were made as *one*. Woman was not created as a new separate species. She came out of man, so she is neither independent of nor separate from man. But now, Paul continues, neither is man independent or separate from woman, because he is born of woman.

Paul's point is that *together* they are human, humanity is one, and we need symbols (like head coverings) to remind us of this incredible mystery. Paul refers to angels in this passage,

[16] Matthew 28:19
[17] Colossians 1:16

because this profound and mysterious truth is not only on display for us to understand and marvel at, it is there for the unseen realm to see and wonder at as well. For man to tangibly and publicly acknowledge his source, and for woman to do the same, is to declare that we are one—one with the Godhead, and one with each other. None of the relationships mentioned in this letter to the Corinthians are there to point out very separate roles as individuals, nor are they to point out their rank or their worth with respect to a hierarchy. These relationships are mentioned to point out their *oneness*, that they each come from and go to the other. If we read this passage through the lens of division (the understanding that we are separate, independent beings), then all we take from it is instructions about how to order and compare ourselves with one another in a state of separation. But, amazingly, this is a text to remind us of the oneness of humankind, and our oneness with the Godhead.

When the Son came to dwell among humankind, we find he also taught and modelled that we are to humbly and mutually serve one another, not wrestle for rank and position. "The rulers of the Gentiles lord it over them," he said, "and their superiors exercise authority over them. It shall not be this way among you...whoever wants to be first among you must be your slave."[18] The Son came to humankind to serve, not to be served, to give his life as a ransom for others, and to impart his giftings and authority to others.[19] His message was and is that *no one* should rule over *any* another, but all should live in mutual surrender and empowerment.

[18] Matthew 20:25-28
[19] Luke 9:1

Back in the garden the commission to rule was given to both the man and the woman with no disclaimer and no divvying up of duties. We also understand that contained in the first man and woman was all of humanity, and so the commission to rule was given to the man, the woman, and to their children, and to every generation to follow. One of the first consequences of humankind's choice to eat from the tree of the knowledge of good and evil came to Eve, and it has impacted male and female relationships ever since. God tells her that from now on, her desire would be for (or 'contrary to' in some translations) her husband but that he would rule over her. What was meant to be a relationship of joint rulership suddenly became one with conflicting wills and wrangling for position. Right now it is not even really possible for us to think in any other terms than ranking and jockeying for position since it has been hard-wired into us, as it were. But, in order to rule well, in the way that God originally designed, we need the whole. This means we need men, we need women, and we actually need children, too.

God could have arranged it so that the following generations of men and women would come into the world as fully formed adults—he is God after all. But he did not; he specifically designed children. They are not an accidental piece in this story. Infancy and childhood are not unfortunate stages that we all need to get through as quickly as possible so we can finally arrive at adulthood and have something of worth to contribute to the greater whole. Children are designed by God, so they, too, have a place in the family and a very unique voice in the community.

Children see and receive the world through such different eyes than adults: remarkably honest, receptive, trusting, and expectant eyes. Children are still learning who they are and how to understand and relate to the world. For infants and young children especially, filters for their understandings or their behaviours have not yet fully developed. They have not yet learned how to control or mask what is going on inside of them, nor have they yet learned filters of politeness or protection in order to control what they say or do in response to what they observe or experience. Watching and listening to children in our world teaches us far more about ourselves than we realize, or maybe are willing to admit. Their behaviour and their responses visibly demonstrate what they are receiving and absorbing from us and from the community in which they find themselves.

Children who are confident and kind reflect that they have been seen, heard, and loved, and their expectation (the filter through which they see their world) is then that others will see, hear, and love them. When they find others who do not, these children have a safe haven to return to with voices who can help them understand and respond appropriately and effectively to these confusing new situations (whether these voices are immediate caregivers or not). Children who are aggressive or perhaps emotionally detached, reflect that something in their world is not right. Filters are being formed—perhaps a filter which says they must fight to be seen or heard by others, or perhaps a filter that says they had best shut down emotions or disconnect because connection results in pain that they are not yet capable of dealing with.

Infants and children are looking to others to help them emotionally regulate, so when they cannot, it tells us what is missing or needed in the world around them. The voice that children bring to the community can be a gauge to help us see our own dysfunctions, and those in our families, our churches, or our societies. Recognizing, receiving, and protecting this voice should absolutely be a focus of our attention and ministry. As Christians we must ask ourselves: do we see and hear the children in our churches, our ministries, or in the societies around us, and are we engaging with them and offering havens of safety to help them build filters of confidence and kindness?

Children are not only a gift to help us gauge the health of our communities, like men and women they, too, can receive from the Godhead and bring needed truth and guidance to communities. With their honest, clear, trusting, and expectant eyes, children can sometimes catch the voice of God where disappointment, selfishness, or rebellion may have blocked the ears of adults.

Eli was a priest and judge during the time when kings had not yet been appointed in Israel. He was not only supposed to be the go-between for Israel and God, he was also supposed to be a leader that brought earthly salvation to the people of Israel. Yet, because of the sin of his adult sons and his refusal to do anything about it, Eli had lost touch with the first voice. In this circumstance, God was, as always, looking for someone who could and would listen and respond to his voice, even if appointed priests and leaders could not. He chose little Samuel. Even though Samuel could not detect the voice of God initially, Eli had enough wisdom to recognize that God was speaking to the boy and so he instructed him to respond to the voice. Samuel did respond and God continued to speak. And so here we find God speaking to a priest and judge of Israel, through a child. What Samuel prophesied to Eli came to be exactly as he declared it, and as he grew, "the LORD was with him, and let none of his words fall to the ground".[20] God is not concerned about gender, nor is he concerned about age; he simply speaks to whoever is listening.

It is to everyone's benefit that we give place and value to the voice of children in our worlds. We also need to remember that Jesus tells us we must become like them if we want to enter the kingdom of heaven. Considering again the central place that unity has in the heart and purposes of God, we as Christians (especially those in leadership) must ask ourselves how we give value and place in our communities to each of these voices—men, women, and children.

The longer I walk with God and with others, the more grateful I become for the wider body of Christ that I find myself in. I find his voice all throughout this vast body, helping me to discover so much more of the profound mysteries of the seen and unseen worlds. The more I dive into diverse community and seek to find and receive the voice of God from the different members within it—male or female, young or old, local or expat, rich or poor—the more I realize how little I personally know and understand of the Godhead, really how little *any* of us knows and understands. The truth is that neither I, nor you, nor anyone will ever have the full and complete picture of God until we actually see him. In the meantime, perhaps the most profound, life-giving truth that we could ever have

[20] 1 Samuel 3:19

been given is 'Immanuel' meaning 'God with us'. God is with us even though we do not fully know or understand him. The truth of Immanuel brings the realization that we do not actually need the whole complete picture in order for him to be with us. We do not need to have *all* the right beliefs, or perform *all* the right practices in order to be one with him. All we need is to listen to and believe the voice of the Spirit, to partake of the life blood of his Son, to surrender and commit fully to relationship with the Godhead, even if we do not yet fully know what that will all entail. If we choose to receive his provision, given so that we can become forever part of the divine family, then we *are* part of this family. We can be one with him, and one with each other. Glorious truth!

11

On Earth As It Is In Heaven

All our lives belong to thee,
Thou our final loyalty;
Slaves are we whene'er we share
That devotion anywhere.
God of love and God of power.
Thou hast called us for this hour.
—Gerald H. Kennedy[1]

Alone we can do so little, together we can do so much.
—Helen Keller

Desire and pursuit of the whole requires our vision to expand dramatically. When we are looking forward to the final chapter of our current story—the great future wedding of the church to the Son, the new Jerusalem, the tree of life, and even the necessary judgment—we cannot simply be content with only being introduced to God, or with only introducing

[1] Job R, Shawchuck N. *A Guide To Prayer*. Nashville, TN: Upper Room; 1988.

others to him. We must press on to really know him and surrender all, and we must walk alongside others to encourage them to do the same. We must discover and throw off all that hinders anything but total commitment to him, and to full restoration of perfect unity. Jesus did not call for and was never satisfied with anything less than total and complete surrender. His invitation was a call to leave *everything*, to sell *everything*, to come and *die*. Full surrender is the only way to be one with him and one with each other. Pursuit of the whole requires us to go deeper into ourselves and into our communities than many of us have understood or have been accustomed to.

Paul understood and embraced this invitation to come and die. He died to his own success, the protection of his reputation, his fleshly desires, even his own will, all for the glory set before him. He declared that he counted all things as loss for the sake of knowing Jesus. He wanted to know Jesus and the power of his resurrection, to share in his sufferings, to become conformed to him in his death, to be one with him.[2] Paul wanted to take hold of that for which the Son took hold of him, that being the heavenward calling,[3] which is the final chapter of this current story. He knew that he had not yet laid hold of it, but he was pressing and straining ahead in pursuit of the whole. He was heading towards this prize.

Paul not only embraced this invitation to come and die, he also always invited others to do the same, and he actively battled in prayer for those he invited to come wholeheartedly to Jesus. His desire was that they also would be able to make it through to the incredible final chapter of this current story,

[2] Philippians 3:10-11
[3] Philippians 3:14

where full and perfect connection will finally be restored. Paul likened his wrestling for Christ to be fully formed in those that he had preached to, with the pains of childbirth.[4] He was not content with merely testifying about Jesus to others: he wanted Jesus *in* them. It was just as Jesus prayed, "that they may all be one, just as you, Father, are in me, and I in you, that they also may be in us."[5] Real and total unity is simply not possible without surrender to the only One found worthy. We submit to him and his standard so that humble, mutual submission to one another may also be possible. Have we not tasted and seen that God is good so that we, too, are willing and ready to fully come and die? Will we not now invite others to do the same and wrestle with them until we all attain such maturity, and in so doing find real life and true community?

Expanding our vision not only requires us to go deeper; it also requires us to go much wider. In our pursuit of the whole we must look beyond our small, comfortable communities to see the greater body of Christ. I feel so privileged to live where I do as I am regularly amazed at the incredible people in the wider body of Christ that I get to meet. One such example is an Iranian couple, who was a part of our ministry training program for one year. As part of a course on listening prayer and inner healing, I was teaching a class on forgiveness where time and space was given for participants to go and talk directly with God. They were invited to ask God about who they might need to forgive, and what he wanted to restore to them as they released others from their debts by handing those debts and judgment over to God.

[4] Galatians 4:19
[5] John 17:21

When we came back together as a class, this couple shared that they had come to a decision: they needed to forgive a man in Iran who was still in prison because he had defrauded them. According to Iranian law, he would remain there until his debts were paid or unless the complainants chose to release him. At the first scheduled holiday in our program, the husband returned to Iran for a few days and had this man released from prison. He then met with the man's parents (who had previously contacted them, asking for mercy) in a park with the documents of release, a cake, and an open explanation as to why he and his wife had chosen to do such a thing. We get to encounter such stories of strength and compassion in the body of Christ when we begin to look just a little beyond our immediate contexts.

Expanding our vision in pursuit of the whole requires us to begin looking even to those who maybe do not yet know that they are called to be a part of the greater body of Christ. Another reason I feel so privileged to live where I do and meet the people I do is because I regularly get to witness how far the love of God reaches to call out his bride from all corners.

I will never forget the Yezidi family that we met one evening at the Ankara bus terminal. They had just arrived in Turkey and needed help to get in touch with the UNHCR and to find a place to stay while they applied for refugee status. I had just moved out of my apartment but still had it for a full month, with utilities not yet turned off, and so we brought this family of ten to stay there initially. We welcomed them into our world and got to know them quite well. One brother in the family had heard a voice back in northern Iraq telling him that they needed to leave their town, and quickly. His wife thought he was crazy, but as things got more dangerous, they finally left together with his parents and siblings.

Not long after they left, Isis stormed their home in the Sinjar valley, mass killing and taking many captive. Those who managed to flee were then trapped on a mountain without food or water for many days before any help could come. The day of the attack we just sat and wept together with this family as they were on their phones getting updates from friends or relatives who were still in that region as events unfolded. By this point we had shared much together. They had taught us about the Yezidi faith and we also shared about our Christian faith. Later on, this one brother who had heard the voice telling them to leave, and his wife, each had an encounter with Jesus, and they decided they wanted to follow him. It was then that they understood who the voice was that had been telling them to leave their home. That first voice from the garden had been calling to this family, and when they responded, he led them straight to us.

This pursuit of the whole brings us into a task that is so much greater than anything we have ever been a part of before and something so far beyond our capabilities or our scope that it forces us to look beyond ourselves. There are many who do not know God but who desire and are in pursuit of unity. This is amazing because those who obey God's principles (even without knowing it) will indeed reap the benefits of his provision. "A harvest of righteousness is sown in peace by those who make peace."[6] John Lennon in his famous song imagined a world with *no borders, no killing or dying, no possessions, no greed, a world living as one.* But it was nothing more than

6 James 3:18

imagination, because we did not, have not, and simply will not see this vision realized if it lacks God. A pursuit of the whole that has a vision only for a whole humanity (not a humanity that is reconciled to God) can never achieve true unity no matter how much hope or passion or sacrifice there may be. This is because such a pursuit is lacking the most essential piece: the source and sustainer of all life and the only One good.

Whenever any two independent wills come together, if there is no central standard to unify them, their wills will be opposed at one point or another, or maybe on all points. Outside of the central standard for good and evil given by the Godhead, humankind can only, and will only ever be divided and broken.

As we look to God's standard and to his provision, we recognize the difficulty, indeed impossibility of this pursuit of the whole. But we also increasingly discover the many others who are also after him and his glory and actively seeking to unite with others, who are surrendered to him no matter their background. This God-given desire for and pursuit of the whole not only expands our vision to believe for it, it also allows us to see it, since this pursuit puts us in direct connection with it. When unity becomes our desire and focus, we inevitably find so much more of God, and we also inevitably find those who are longing for and pursuing the glorious whole. Together, we can become so much more than we ever were, or ever could be separately. In learning to die to self and grow in love, we can together anticipate and prepare for the day when we will finally be fully united as one, with the Godhead and with each other.

The ending to our story is really only the beginning of a new one. Our story began in a garden where humankind was given the unique mandate to rule because they had been created in the image of God. Humankind was made as flesh but was invited to partake of the eternal. They were invited to eat from the tree of life to receive everlasting life, but were also given the opportunity to refuse. This was an invitation to *voluntarily* surrender to God, to *choose* the way of love. In doing so, humankind would have then been able to rule in the way that God would rule this world, with love and in unity, and for all eternity. But humankind did not choose the tree of life. We chose to decide for ourselves what is best. We chose the flesh and so chose division and destruction. But God made provision for unity to still be possible. He gave us his voice. He gave us recorded testimonies, promises, and instructions. He gave us himself. God did not have to, and certainly did not need to, but he *chose* to submit himself to his own creation. The Creator chose to be subjected to centuries of rejection and hurt by a people he loved so extravagantly by sharing his sovereignty with them, and allowing them to choose. Then he chose to subject the Son (who in turn chose to submit himself) to horrific suffering, rejection, and death. All of this happened as a result of the rebellion of the created. But God did all of this to counter that rebellion with submission. He subjected himself to suffering and took it all on as if it were his own so that we might be one with him and one with each other.

Through the sacrifice and blood of the Son and through the empowerment and fellowship of the Spirit, a new humanity is being formed: one that is not born of the flesh or of the will of man, but one born of spirit and of the will of God, one that can fully love and be loved, and truly live as one. It is fitting that in the last chapter of the Bible we return to the garden:

> Then the angel showed me the river of the water of life, bright as crystal, flowing from the throne of God and of the Lamb through the middle of the street of the city; also, on either side of the river, the tree of life with its twelve kinds of fruit, yielding its fruit each month. The leaves of the tree were for the healing of the nations.[7]

The Bible begins with the tree of life in the garden which humankind was banished from after choosing to eat of the tree of the knowledge of good and evil. Now we see access to the tree of life restored: the fruit of which brings healing. Now at last can humankind return to paradise to eternally enjoy the abundance of a relationship they were called to enjoy from the very beginning.

I want to leave you with the beauty and hope found in the lyrics of a hymn I have come to love. It was written by Nathan Partain in "an effort to depict the church as she really is in Christ, indwelt by the Holy Spirit,...to describe the beauty of her holiness and the intimacy of her love and relationship with her God,...[and] to be another sung-prayer added to the thousands of years of prayers that the church has cried out, 'Come, Lord Jesus!'"[8]

---

[7] Revelation 22:1-2

[8] Partainwordsandmusic V. Your Beloved is Ready. Nathan Partain. https://partainwordsandmusic.wordpress.com/2014/01/27/your-beloved-is-ready/. Published 2020. Accessed June 25, 2020.

Your Beloved Is Ready

Verse 1

She has saved her whole heart for you, Lord,
She has kept her eyes pure for you, Lord.
She has waited and waited, while her hungers were raging,
To taste only the love of her Lord.

She has set her delight in you, Lord,
She has stayed all her thoughts on you, Lord.
She has stilled her desires, all her tossing and straying,
She has put all her hope in you, Lord.

Chorus:
You have washed her for the day of her wedding,
Promised yourself, by your Spirit abiding.
In the earthquakes and war, Lord, can you hear her singing,
Her arms are raised high, she is radiant, she is holy,
Your beloved is ready.

Verse 2

She has shut out the greed of her soul,
Scoffs at scarcity, rotting and mold.
She has given so freely, to the mean and unworthy,
She's so loved that she cannot withhold.

She surrendered her fight for control,
She has waived every right that she holds.
She wiped out all the debts that she'd demanded from others,
Cause she knew that she'd owed so much more.

Verse 3

She has torn up her murderous laws,
Her comparing and searching for flaws.
But you've made her so humble, holding others so highly,
That her joy has been filled to the full.

She took off her pretense for you, Lord,
She confessed all her shame to you, Lord.
She came out of her hiding, to be known so profoundly,
She's so free she can dance for you, Lord.

CPSIA information can be obtained
at www.ICGtesting.com
Printed in the USA
LVHW111747150421
684631LV00008B/1696